SPORT FISH OF NORTH AMERICA POCKET GUIDE

Produced in cooperation with Wildlife Forever

by Ann E. McCarthy, Director of Education

Adventure Publications, Inc.
Cambridge, Minnesota

DEDICATION

To DHG, Jack, Ron, Babe, Scott, Zim and all those passion
about fishing, committed to conservation and dedicated to you

– Ann E. McCa

Special thanks to the Zimmerman Group for their friendship, s
port and expertise.

Thanks, also, to Kathy Corser, Junior Angler Program Coordina
and the International Game Fish Association (IGFA) for its co
butions to this product and to their steadfast devotion to sport
fishing and aquatic resource conservation. Contact IGFA
www.igfa.org or 954-927-2628.

Thanks to the National Fresh Water Fishing Hall of Fa
(NFWFHF) for their contributions and support of fishing
aquatic resources. Contact NFWFHF at www.freshwater-fishing
or (715) 634-4440.

Research and Editorial Assistance: David A. Frederick

Cover and Book Design: Jonathan Norberg

Illustration Credits: Joseph Tomelleri (color illustrations) and B
Doll (line art illustration on page 8).

This publication was funded in part by ACT II Microwave Popc
and Jiffy Pop Popcorn, which are manufactured by Golden Va
Microwave Foods, a division of ConAgra Foods, Inc.

Second Printing
Copyright 2001 by Wildlife Forever
Published by Adventure Publications, Inc.
820 Cleveland St. S
Cambridge, MN 55008, 1-800-678-7006
Printed in China

bOUT WILDLIFE FOREVER

dlife Forever is a nonprofit conservation organization
dicated to conserving America's wildlife heritage through
ucation, preservation of habitat and management of fish
d wildlife. Working at the grassroots level, Wildlife Forever
F) has completed conservation projects in all 50 states.
has also initiated several new and innovative outreach
grams including the Wildlife Forever State-Fish Art
oject, Handicapped Americans for Wildlife Conservation
AWC), Masters Walleye Circuit, Racing for Wildlife and
Teddy Roosevelt Conservation Alliance.

of the Wild

*e "cry of the wild" can still be heard across this great land. I
ve heard the bugle of an elk amid the foothills of the western
ins...the shrill of a bald eagle along the banks of the mighty
ssissippi...the roar of a brown bear on windswept tundra...the
nder of migrating waterfowl on coastal shores...the crow of a
asant on Midwestern farm fields...the gobble of a wild turkey
ong eastern hardwoods and the haunting cry of a sandhill
ne in the wetlands of the Central Flyway. America is truly
ssed. A land rich in natural resources, much of our identity and
ture can be attributed to the natural world. The legacy of our
ural resource heritage must be preserved.*

*ope this book will provide you with an insight to the many won-
s of the natural world and serve as a stepping-stone to the great
doors.*

rs in wildlife...forever,

glas H. Grann
sident & CEO, Wildlife Forever

To learn more contact us at 763-253-0222,
2700 Freeway Blvd., Ste. 1000, Brooklyn Center, MN 5543
or check out our website at www.wildlifeforever.org.

ABOUT THE ILLUSTRATOR

"As a kid, I loved nothing better than to spend a day nosi around a lake or stream," illustrator Joseph Tomelleri co ments. "My illustrations grew out of a love for fishing and the environment that surrounded the fishes. Most bodies water are mysterious; you never know just exactly what lur below the surface, and that's intriguing." His remarkable fi illustrations have appeared in magazines such as *Field Stream* and *Outdoor Life*, books, identification guides a newspapers as well as on greeting cards, posters and t-shir

Joseph catches live fish to study before drawing them in c ored pencil. "The illustrations might take anywhere fro eight to seventy hours to complete," Joseph says, "a they're all drawn from real fishes, which takes most of t guesswork out of drawing." Joseph's illustrations are ve precise and accurately portray the colors, scales and fins each fish. Many ichthyologists (scientists that study fis regard Joseph Tomelleri as the finest scientific illustrator fish in the world. To see more of Joseph's wonderful artwo visit his website at www.americanfishes.com.

ABOUT THE WILDLIFE FOREVER STATE-FISH ART PROJECT

The Wildlife Forever State-Fish Art Project is an excitir multi-media education program designed to use art as means of increasing awareness of and respect for fish a aquatic resources. The project culminates in a national contest for children in grades 4-12 where children subr drawings of their state fish. For more information about t Wildlife Forever State-Fish Art Project contact them www.statefishart.com. See examples of past winners on t next page.

WF State-Fish Art Project Past Winners

Grades 4-6: **John Parisi** of Philadelphia, Pennsylvania *(Brook Trout)*

Grades 7-9: **Matt Rudolph** of Granger, Indiana *(Largemouth Bass)*

Grades 10-12: **Matt Mullen** of Green River, Wyoming *(Cutthroat Trout)*

FROM BABE WINKELMAN

Dear Friends,

I hope this book will spark the sense of wonder all childr
have for the natural world and lead to a genuine apprec
tion and understanding of all things wet and wild a
ultimately to a lifelong connection to fish and wildlife.

As Honorary Chairman of Wildlife Forever's State-Fish
Project, it is my sincere wish that this book will serve parer
youth group leaders and educators as a tool for children
learn about the wonders of our wild world beyond the cc
fines of the classroom.

This guide describes some truly amazing characteristics
fish and provides a brief introduction to the fascinat
world of fishing.

Wet a line soon, and enjoy *Sport Fish of North America*!

Good fishing,

Babe Winkelman

Babe Winkelman

TABLE OF CONTENTS

About Wildlife Forever 3

About the Illustrator 4

About the Wildlife Forever State-Fish Art Project 4

From Babe Winkelman 6

About Fish 8

Safety 10

About Fishing 10

Basics of Catch-and-Release 11

About This Book 12

Fish 14-112

Fish and Wildlife Agencies 114

Catch List 120

Glossary of Terms 127

Highlights of Wildlife Forever's
National Fisheries Projects 135

About Fish

More than 22,000 species of fish live in the world's wa
and roughly 2,000 live in North America alone. Of the
only about 60 are sport fish. Sport fish are certain species
fish that anglers actively pursue because they are good to
or are considered fun and challenging to catch. The 50 sp
fish in this book are some of North America's most popu

There are flat fish, skinny fish and fish that crawl on lar
flying fish, electric fish and fish that live in schools. Sor
have stripes and spots, while others glow with all the colʊ
of the rainbow. The tremendous diversity among fish resʊ
from 400 million years of adaptation and unique conditiʊ
associated with life in the water. The oldest group of verʊ
brates, fish can be found wherever there is watʊ
Three-quarters of the Earth's surface is covered by eitʊ
salt water or fresh water.

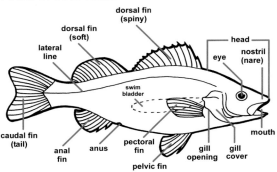

Parts of a Fish

Gills are thin membranes located inside slit-like openinʊ
behind the head. Fish get oxygen from the water by pullʊ
it through their mouths and over their gills.

...ns help a fish to balance and move in the water, and each ... has a particular function. The **pectoral fins** help with ...ing, swimming to the surface and remaining stationary in ... water. These fins are found behind the gills. The **dorsal** ... keeps the fish from rolling and stands up from the back. **...lvic fins** stabilize the fish and help it to balance. The **anal** ... helps with balance and is located near the rear of the ...lly. The **caudal fin** or tail propels and steers the fish. A ...ked tail allows for increased speed, while a broad tail ...ows for increased maneuverability.

...ost fish have a flexible armor of protective **scales** covering ...eir bodies. Scales, which vary in size and shape, are ...ated with a slimy layer of mucous that has antiseptic prop-...ies which protects the fish against disease and parasites.

...most all fish have a **swim bladder**, which is a balloon-like ...gan in the gut area. The swim bladder helps the fish to ...gulate its buoyancy. Fish also have a row of pores called ... **lateral line** in their skin. The pores are connected to a ...ries of nerves which are very sensitive to vibrations. The ...eral line extends from just behind the head along the ...dy to the tail on either side of the fish and detects slight ...ovements of water, which helps the fish to avoid danger or ...capture prey.

...mouflage

...ost fish have some kind of protective coloring called *cam-...flage* which enables them to blend in with their ...rroundings. Many are patterned with bars, stripes or ...ots. *Counter shading*, also called *obliterative*, is a very ...mmon type of camouflage and means the fish has darker ...oring on its back and lighter coloring on its belly. Counter ...ading helps conceal fish from predators above such as ...ld eagles and predators below such as other fish.

Types of Fish

Fish are divided into two groups. *Chondrichthyes* cons primarily of marine species and includes sharks, skates a rays. They have a skeleton made of flexible cartilage rath than bone, and their mouths and gill openings are on t undersides of their bodies. *Osteichthyes*, by far the large group, includes all fish that have a skeleton made of bo such as trout, sunfish, perch, salmon, walleye and ba: Scientists define a small third group of fish called *Agnat* to classify a few primitive species including the lamprey.

The Name Game

There are paddlefish, porcupine fish, sunfish, parrot fis dog fish, goat fish and even butterfly fish. Although fish ha many distinguishing characteristics such as shape, size a color, species identification can be tricky because people different regions call fish different names. For examp largemouth bass, bigmouth bass, black bass, green ba and bayou bass are all names used to identify the sar fish, the *Micropterus salmoides*. Every fish has only one s entific name, no matter how many common names it ha

SAFETY

Use common sense when you go fishing. Handle hooks a lures with care – they're very sharp! Try to find fishing spc away from busy roads, and don't go fishing by yourse Whenever you fish from a boat or dock, always wear your li jacket.

ABOUT FISHING

Young and old alike, one in four Americans fish. People f to spend time with family and friends or to get in touch w nature. They fish for sporting challenge and to find "the o that got away."

strict guidelines exist to ensure fishing success.
ccessful anglers experiment with different tackle, technol-
y and techniques. A little bit of luck also never hurts. Many
ngs affect whether or not the fish are biting, including
ter temperature, time of day, weather, location and season.

hing for freshwater and saltwater sport fish requires
rtsmanship, ethics and etiquette. Responsible anglers
pect each other and the resources they use, maintain
an waterways and obey all laws and regulations. As con-
vationists, they practice catch-and-release.

hing regulations, including fishing seasons, creel limits
d methods, are defined and enforced by each state's gov-
ment. Each year, the millions of dollars generated by the
es of fishing licenses and equipment provides funds for
neries management projects. To learn more about fishing,
te regulations, outdoor safety and conservation, contact
r state agency. Many fish and wildlife agencies offer edu-
ional classes. Contact information can be found on
es 114-119.

ASICS OF CATCH-AND-RELEASE

tch-and-release refers to catching a fish and releasing it
e. Catch-and-release is sometimes voluntary and some-
es mandatory depending on the species caught, size,
e of year and location. Catch-and-release benefits fish
ulations by protecting healthy breeding adults.

Hints for successful catch-and-release

- Land the fish quickly
- Ask for assistance if necessary
- Don't let the fish bounce along the dock, boat or shore
- Wet hands before handling the fish and handle it as
  little as possible

- Keep the fish in the water as much as possible
- Hold the fish firmly but do not squeeze
- Support the fish by placing a hand under its belly
- Use a needle-nose pliers to remove the hook by pulling in the opposite direction of the hook point
- Cut the line in a deeply-hooked fish
- Cradle the fish in the water until it is able to swim

ABOUT THIS BOOK

Sensitive, Threatened or Endangered Species

Some of the fish in this book are listed as sensitive, threaten or endangered by the U.S. Fish and Wildlife Servi Placement on this list is a result of a declining population o particular species. Habitat loss, pollution, dams and dise are major causes of declining fish populations and may aff one or more areas. It is possible for a fish to be endanger in one part of its range and plentiful in another.

Regulations for sensitive, threatened or endangered fish v by state and region. Depending on the area in which you fi catch-and-release for a particular fish might be mandator is important to check with your local fish and wildlife office regulations that apply to these species.

Sensitive means declining population, in danger of beco ing threatened; **Threatened** means seriously declin population, close to becoming endangered; **Endanger** means critically declining population, close to becom extinct. If a fish falls into one of these categories it is no under the Did You Know heading.

Records

The International Game Fish Association (IGFA) verifies wo record catches and promotes education for young angle

t of their mission is to maintain fishing standards and rules.
e National Fresh Water Fishing Hall of Fame (NFWFHF) is
educational museum organization founded to promote the
rt of freshwater fishing. They verify national records.
cords from both organizations were utilized in order to find
largest North American catch.

ns

e icons on each page show you which of the three types
bait to use for each fish. Some fish will take all three kinds;
ers may only take one or two. Natural baits are part of a
's natural diet and may include worms, leeches, min-
vs, grasshoppers and crickets. Processed baits are items
h as bits of cheese, processed meats, bread and com-
rcial products such as Powerbait. Lures are a type of
ficial bait made to imitate natural bait; many kinds exist,
uding spoons, jigs, spinners and plugs.

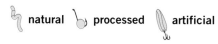

natural   processed   artificial

es

ce there are so many kinds of lures, we have pictured a
of the major types below. You don't have to have all or
of these to catch fish; lures are only one kind of bait.

Buzzbait	Jerkbait	Flies	Spoons
Spinners	Jigs	Crankbait	Spinnerbait
Plugs	Plastic worms/insects		

IGFA World Record: No IGFA World Record or NFWFHF Record available. Certified State Record: 17 lbs. 4¼ oz., Billy O' Berry, Polk County, Florida, USA, 1986

DID YOU KNOW? A feisty predator, the Florida Largemouth Bass uses the cover of rocks, timbers, piers and weeds as a hideout while waiting to ambush its prey. A subspecies of the largemouth bass, it grows quickly in its warm water environment often approaching record weight. Bass can be finicky eaters, so anglers frequently switch bait to attract them. The Florida Largemouth Bass is the freshwater state fish of Florida.

natural   artificial

BASS, FLORIDA LARGEMOUTH
Micropterus salmoides floridanus

Common Names: Florida bass, bucketmouth, linesides, green trout, black bass and Oswego bass

Size: average 2-8 lbs.; up to 25" in length

Habitat: estuaries, reservoirs, lakes and ponds with firm, sandy bottoms

Range: native to Florida; also stocked in Texas and California

Food: fish, amphibians (frogs and salamanders), snakes and invertebrates (e.g. earthworms and insects)

Mating: early each spring the male uses its tail to create a saucer-shaped nesting area along the shoreline; the female lays as many as 25,000 eggs; the male fertilizes the eggs and guards the nest and the young, which become fingerlings in 3-6 days

Description: overall greenish in color with a dark lateral line, lighter undersides and diamond-shaped vertical bars on sides; notched fin along the back

Bait: natural bait including worms; various lures including crankbait, spinnerbait, jigs, surface plugs and buzzbait

Life span: about 10 years

IGFA World Record: 3 lbs.11 oz., Allen Christenson, Jr. Lake Travis, Austin, Texas, USA, Sept. 25, 1983

DID YOU KNOW? Commonly classified as a black bass, the Guadalupe Bass is actually a member of the sunfish family. I feeds by capturing its prey and swallowing it headfirst or by taking a large gulp of water to consume all the tiny plants and animals it contains. The Guadalupe Bass is the state fish of Texas.

 natural **artificial**

BASS, GUADALUPE
Micropterus treculii

ommon Names: black bass and Guadalupe spotted bass

Size: average less than 1 lb.; up to 16" in length

Habitat: creeks and medium rivers

Range: native only to Texas; introduced in Colorado

Food: fish and invertebrates (e.g. earthworms and insects)

Mating: each spring and summer the male builds a gravel nest; the female lays up to 9,000 eggs; the male fertilizes the eggs and guards the nest and young

escription: greenish in color with 10-12 dark bars along its sides

Bait: various natural baits including worms, minnows, leeches and crayfish; lures including spinners, spoons, crankbait and plastic worms

Life span: about 7 years

IGFA World Record: 22 lbs. 4 oz., George W. Perry, Montgomery Lake, Georgia, USA, June 2, 1932

DID YOU KNOW? The largemouth bass is very territorial, building nests 30 or more feet apart. This bass may be seen taking bait and then jumping up and shaking its head to dislodge the hook. It has excellent color vision but is sensitive to light and sudden drops in water temperature. It becomes so inactive in cold water that divers have been known to swim up and touch this fish. The largemouth bass is the state fish of Georgia and Mississippi, the freshwater state fish of Alabama, and the state sport fish of Tennessee.

 natural **artificial**

BASS, LARGEMOUTH
Micropterus salmoides

Common Names: black bass, green bass, bigmouth, linesides, northern largemouth and bucketmouth

Size: average 1-6 lbs.; up to 21" in length

Habitat: swamps, sloughs, slow-moving rivers, lakes and ponds with heavy cover (brush, sunken logs and rocks)

Range: throughout U.S. including the Great Lakes and Mississippi River Valley south to the Gulf

Food: mostly fish; also crustaceans (e.g. crayfish), amphibians (frogs and salamanders), insects, ducklings and snakes; feeds more heavily as water temperature warms

Mating: each spring the male creates a 2-3' nest by shaking his head and tail near heavy cover; the female lays as many as 43,000 eggs; the male guards the eggs and young for about a month

Description: black to olive in color with dark wavy band running the length of the sides; upper jaw extends beyond eye

Bait: natural baits including worms, minnows, leeches; various lures including crankbait, spinnerbait, jigs, plastic worms, jigging spoons and buzzbait

Life span: about 15 years

IGFA World Record: 3 lbs. 0 oz., Peter Gulgin, York Rive
Ontario, Canada, Aug. 1, 1974

DID YOU KNOW? The rock bass can be tough to sp
against its background. It can actually change its pigmenta
tion in a matter of minutes to provide good camouflage.
highly adaptable fish, the prolific Rock Bass is actually
member of the sunfish family.

 natural **artificial**

BASS, ROCK
Ambloplites rupestris

Common Names: black perch, goggle-eye and rock sunfish

Size: average 1 lb.; up to 18" in length

Habitat: lakes, ponds and streams

Range: northeastern U.S. west through the Great Lakes and the Mississippi River Valley south to the Gulf

Food: crustaceans (e.g. crayfish), insects and fish

Mating: spawning activity occurs early each summer; the male constructs a nest usually near heavy cover; the female lays approximately 5,000 eggs; the male guards the nest and young

Description: dark olive-brown in color with irregular dark vertical stripes and lighter undersides; bluish black-tipped gill cover; red eyes and forked tail

Bait: natural baits including worms, small crayfish and minnows; various lures including jigs, crankbait, spinners and spoons

Life span: about 10-12 years

IGFA World Record: 10 lbs. 14 oz., John T. Gorman, Dale Hollow, Tennessee, USA, Apr. 24, 1969

DID YOU KNOW? Native to North America, the Smallmouth Bass is the second largest member of the sunfish family. A highly prized sport fish, the Smallmouth Bass is well known for its scrappy disposition and fighting character when caught by anglers. In fact, a famous quote from the 1800s describes this fish as "inch for inch and pound for pound the gamest fish that swims."

 natural artificial

BASS, SMALLMOUTH
Micropterus dolomieu

Common Names: black bass, smallie, redeye, brownie, brown bass, smallmouth and bronzeback

Size: average 1-3 lbs.; up to 15" in length

Habitat: clear, quiet streams with gravel or rocky bottoms and abundant shade; deep lakes and reservoirs with rocky shoals

Range: northern states; heavily stocked in the southern states including Texas, Tennessee, Georgia, North Carolina, South Carolina, Arkansas and Alabama

Food: small fish, crustaceans (e.g. crayfish) and nymph larvae (immature insects)

Mating: each spring or early summer the male builds a nest often near a log or boulder; the female lays 5,000-14,000 eggs; the male protects the eggs and young for 3-4 weeks

Description: color varies, includes brown, bronze, golden brown or olive with lighter undersides; red eyes and a protruding jaw

Bait: natural baits including crayfish, minnows, leeches, worms; various lures including plastic worms

Life span: about 5-6 years

IGFA World Record: 9 lbs. 9 oz., Kirk M. Sakamoto, Pine Flat Lake, California, USA, Oct. 12, 1996

DID YOU KNOW? Unlike other black bass, the Spotted Bass often occurs in groups or schools. It changes color becoming lighter as water clarity decreases. Although they prefer mornings and evenings, bass sometimes start feeding frenzies midday. The Spotted Bass is the state fish of Kentucky.

 natural **artificial**

BASS, SPOTTED
Micropterus punctulatus

Common Names: Kentucky bass, spot and Alabama spotted bass

Size: average 3-5 lbs.; up to 18" in length

Habitat: clear, slow-moving, small to medium-sized streams and deep reservoirs

Range: throughout the U.S. including upper Midwest, Gulf and some western states

Food: small fish, insects and crustaceans (e.g. crayfish)

Mating: each spring the male creates a nest near heavy cover such as brush or logs; the female lays thousands of eggs and the male fertilizes them; the male guards the eggs and young for up to one month

Description: olive green back with dark diamond-shaped blotches and lighter undersides

Bait: natural baits including crayfish, minnows and worms; various lures including crankbait, spinnerbait, jigs and plastic worms

Life span: about 7 years

IGFA World Record: 78 lbs. 8 oz., Albert R. McReynolds, Atlantic City, New Jersey, USA, Sept. 21, 1982

DID YOU KNOW? Within the scientific name of the Striped Bass is the word *saxatilis* which means "rock dweller." Highly prized by anglers for its desirable meat, the Striped Bass has a long history as a significant commercial species, especially on the East Coast. Bass drive schools of small fish to the surface of the water to eat them in a feeding frenzy. The Striped Bass is the state fish of Maryland and South Carolina and the saltwater state fish of New Hampshire.

 natural  **processed** **artificial**

BASS, STRIPED
Morone saxatilis

mmon Names: striper, rockfish and linesides

Size: average 5-10 lbs.; up to 35" in length

Habitat: saltwater as well as freshwater; often found near rock jetties and piers

Range: Atlantic coast, Gulf, Pacific coast and Chesapeake Bay

Food: small fish (e.g. herring, flounder and smelt), eels, invertebrates (e.g. worms and squid), insects and crustaceans (e.g. crabs, lobster and crayfish); heaviest feeding at dawn or dusk; feed in groups

Mating: the Striped Bass is an anadromous species (adults migrate from saltwater to freshwater to mate); however, some Striped Bass live exclusively in freshwater; the female lays as many as 200,000 eggs in light to moderate current; the male fertilizes the eggs; the moving water keeps the eggs afloat until they hatch; up to 50 striped bass may spawn together

scription: bright silver to bluish black in color with 7-8 black unbroken horizontal stripes

Bait: natural bait including worms, processed bait such as cut bait and various lures including spoons and plugs

Life span: about 9 years

IGFA World Record: 6 lbs.13 oz., Ronald L. Sprouse, Lak Orange, Orange, Virginia, USA, July 31, 1989

DID YOU KNOW? Anglers across the south enjoy large cre limits of this fish, which is highly prized for its meat. Althoug the White Bass is incredibly prolific, laying up to one millic eggs, many young do not survive their first year, most fallin prey to other fish. The White Bass is the state fish Oklahoma.

 natural artificial

BASS, WHITE
Morone chrysops

mmon Names: silver bass, striper, sand bass, whitey and dwarf striper

Size: average ½-4 lbs.; up to 15" in length

Habitat: large lakes, reservoirs, ponds and rivers with moderate current

Range: throughout the south, Midwest, Mississippi River Valley, Ohio River Valley and Great Lakes; heavily stocked and transplanted

Food: fish, insects and crustaceans (e.g. shrimp and crayfish); heaviest feeding at dawn or dusk

Mating: each spring the male and female migrate within freshwater rivers to mate; the female lays as many as 1 million eggs; several males gather around the female and fertilize the eggs

scription: silver and dark grayish green in color with 4-10 bold, unbroken horizontal stripes; yellow eyes and protruding lower jaw

Bait: natural bait including shad and minnows; various lures including crankbaits, jigging spoons, buzzbaits, floating plugs and spinners

Life span: about 6 years

IGFA World Record: 2 lbs. 9 oz., John T. Chappell, Duc River, Waverly, Tennessee, USA, Feb. 27, 1998

DID YOU KNOW? The Yellow Bass is highly prized b anglers for its tasty meat and spunky character. Sometimes is considered a pesky pest for it notoriously steals bait fror unsuspecting anglers. The Yellow Bass spawns in schools i open water; the fertilized eggs sink to the bottom to hatch.

 natural artificial

BASS, YELLOW
Morone mississippiensis

mmon Names: barfish, goldbass, yellowjacket and striped bass

Size: average 4 oz.-2 lbs.; up to 18" in length

Habitat: ponds, lakes, rivers, streams and backwaters

Range: Mississippi River Valley, upper Midwest and many southern states; widely stocked

Food: insects, small fish and crustaceans (e.g. crayfish and shrimp)

Mating: each spring the male and female migrate into tributary streams to mate; the female lays 1-2 million eggs and the male fertilizes them

scription: olive-gray back and silvery-yellow sides with several broken stripes

Bait: natural bait including minnows and worms; various lures including jigs, spinners and spoons

ife span: about 4 years

IGFA World Record: 4 lbs. 12 oz., T. S. Hudson, Keton Lake, Alabama, USA, Apr. 9, 1950

DID YOU KNOW? The Bluegill gets its name from the blu coloring on its chin. The male makes a depression for th eggs, waits for the female to come lay eggs and then chase her away while he guards the nest and waits for the eggs t hatch. It has a small mouth so anglers often use a small hoo to facilitate a bite. It is one of the most widely distributed par fish in the U.S. The Bluegill is the state fish of Illinois

 natural artificial

BLUEGILL
Lepomis macrochirus

mmon Names: sun perch, bream, brim, blue sunfish, copperbelly and roach

Size: average less than 1 lb.; up to 10" in length

Habitat: moderately weedy lakes, ponds and slow-moving streams

Range: widely distributed throughout the U.S.; heavily stocked

Food: insects, snails and small fish; sometimes aquatic plants

Mating: each spring the male builds a nest near other bluegill nests; the female lays 2,000-63,000 eggs; the male guards nest and young

scription: yellow to dark blue in color with 5 dark vertical stripes; orange undersides; dark ear flap with no margin

Bait: natural bait including worms, crickets and meal worms; various lures including small jigs and spinners

Life span: about 11 years

IGFA World Record: 7 lbs. 7 oz., Kevin Kelly, Mill Pond Wantagh, Long Island, NY, USA, Aug. 25, 1993

DID YOU KNOW? The Black Bullhead can tolerate high water temperatures, low levels of dissolved oxygen and some pollutants. For that reason, people are advised to limit the number of wild Black Bullhead they eat because of possible contaminants. However, the Black Bullhead is commonly raised commercially in farm ponds and sold to meat markets and restaurants as a delicacy. Bullheads and catfish have a better sense of taste than other fish. They use taste-sensitive cells in their skin and barbels to test food before they eat it.

 natural **processed** **artificial**

BULLHEAD, BLACK
Ameiurus melas

mmon Names: catfish, black catfish, horned pout and yellow belly bullhead

Size: average 1-2 lbs.; up to 24½" in length

Habitat: ponds, backwaters, creeks and rivers

Range: Montana east to the Atlantic and south through the Mississippi River Valley to the Gulf

Food: mollusks (e.g. mussels, clams and snails), plants and fish; feeding mostly at night

Mating: each spring and early summer the female clears away debris and silt to prepare the nest; the male joins the female spawning up to 5 times an hour; the female lays up to 6,000 eggs: the male and female fan the eggs until they hatch

scription: scaleless skin, bronze, brown or yellowish green in color with lighter undersides; squared tail and multiple barbels (whiskers); spawning males are black in color

Bait: processed bait including stinkbait, cheese, meat, bread and cut fish; natural bait including minnows; various lures including plastic worms, spoons, jigs and lightweight spinners

Life span: about 4-5 years

IGFA World Record: 6 lbs. 1 oz., Bobby Triplett, Waterford, New York, USA, Apr. 26, 1998

DID YOU KNOW? Bullheads rarely die of winter kill because they need very little oxygen. They can burrow into the mud during winter, protecting themselves from low temperatures, exposing only their mouth and gills to the water. The Brown Bullhead is prized for its tasty meat and it is commonly grown commercially in farm ponds for restaurants and meat markets.

 natural processed artificial

BULLHEAD, BROWN
Ameiurus nebulosus

Common Names: common bullhead, mudcat, brown catfish, bullpout and horned pout

Size: average 1-3 lbs.; up to 21" in length

Habitat: creeks, large rivers, deep lakes and reservoirs; often stocked in farm ponds

Range: northern Midwest and Great Lakes east to Maine and south to the Gulf

Food: insects, mollusks (e.g. mussels, clams and snails) and crustaceans (e.g. crayfish)

Mating: early each spring the nest is constructed by both the male and female by fanning out a saucer-shaped depression in the sand or mud; the female lays 2,000-10,000 eggs and the male fertilizes them; the young hatch within 6-9 days; both the eggs and the young are guarded for several weeks

Description: scaleless skin, golden brown, brown or olive with scattered dark spots and lighter undersides; squared tail and multiple barbels (whiskers)

Bait: processed bait including stinkbait, cheese, meat, bread and cut fish; natural bait including minnows; various lures including plastic worms, spoons, jigs and lightweight spinners

Life span: about 6-7 years

IGFA World Record: 4 lbs. 4 oz., Emily Williams, Mormon Lake, Arizona, USA, May 11, 1984

DID YOU KNOW? Bullheads can find food by using their great sense of smell. They are often active and feed in evenings. The Yellow Bullhead is less tolerant of silt and muddy water than other bullhead species, preferring clean water with some vegetation. The Yellow Bullhead is a member of the *Ictaluridae* family, which includes the catfish as well. It is the largest family of freshwater fish in North America representing almost 100 different species.

 natural processed artificial

BULLHEAD, YELLOW
Ameiurus natales

Common Names: yellow cat, creek cat and white-whiskered bullhead

Size: usually less than 1 lb., occasionally up to 3 lbs.; up to 7-11" in length

Habitat: ponds, streams, small to large rivers and shallow lakes

Range: across much of central and eastern U.S.

Food: mollusks (e.g. snails), crustaceans (e.g. crayfish and shrimp), insects, small fish and plant material

Mating: late spring to early summer the male and female construct a nest-like depression; the female lays 2,000-6,000 eggs; the male fertilizes the eggs; the male guards the eggs and the young; the young hatch in 5-10 days

Description: scaleless skin, olive, yellowish brown or dark brown in color with lighter undersides; rounded tail, multiple barbels (whiskers) and whitish, yellow or pinkish chin

Bait: processed bait including stinkbait, cheese, meat, bread and cut fish; natural bait including minnows; various lures including plastic worms, spoons, jigs and lightweight spinners

Life span: about 7 years

NFWFHF Record: 57 lbs. 13 oz., David Nikolow, Tidal Basin, Maryland, USA, June 19, 1983

DID YOU KNOW? A member of the minnow family and a relative of the goldfish, the Common Carp is an important food source throughout much of world except North America and Australia. Introduced into the U.S. in the late 1880s, the Common Carp has caused major destruction of aquatic resources because it competes with native species. Some species of carp have scales only along their lateral line, and some don't have scales at all.

 natural **processed**

CARP, COMMON
Cyprinus carpio

mmon Names: king carp

Size: 5-25 lbs.; up to 36" in length

Habitat: small rivers and lakes

Range: across much of U.S.

Food: plant material, invertebrates (e.g. worms), crustaceans (e.g. shrimp and crayfish), insects and mollusks (e.g. snails)

Mating: each spring and summer multiple males and females gather to mate; the females each lay up to 1 million eggs; the males fertilize the eggs; the young hatch in 5-8 days

scription: scaleless head, fully scaled body, gold, olive or brown in color with lighter undersides; reddish lower fins and a barbel (whisker) at either side of the mouth

Bait: processed bait including bread, luncheon meat, potato cubes, chum, doughballs (made from ingredients such as cornmeal or cornflakes and syrup and rolled into a ball) and corn; natural bait including worms

Life span: about 15 years

IGFA World Record: 58 lbs. 0 oz., W. B. Whaley, Santee Cooper Reservoir, South Carolina, USA, July 7, 1964

DID YOU KNOW? A catfish's barbels contain taste organs much like a tongue. When looking for food, they swim so their barbels scrape the bottom. When they find something edible, they quickly turn and attempt to dig it out. The spiny barbs behind their gill slits can produce a nasty sting. The most widely distributed freshwater catfish, the Channel Catfish is the state fish of Kansas, Nebraska, Missouri and Tennessee.

 natural  **processed**

CATFISH, CHANNEL
Ictalurus punctatus

Common Names: spotted cat, blue channel cat, fiddler, spotted catfish, Great Lakes catfish and lady cat

Size: 2-7 lbs.; up to 24" in length

Habitat: streams, rivers, ponds, lakes and reservoirs

Range: central U.S., Great Lakes east to the Atlantic and south to the Gulf

Food: insects, mollusks (e.g. clams and snails), crustaceans (e.g. crayfish and crabs), small fish and plants

Mating: late each spring or early summer the male builds a nest in heavy cover or along the shoreline; the female lays 2,000-20,000 eggs; the male fertilizes the eggs; the male guards the eggs and young

Description: light olive green to pale blue in color with irregular dark spots; deeply forked tail and multiple barbels (whiskers)

Bait: processed baits including doughballs (made from ingredients such as cornmeal or corn-flakes and syrup and rolled into a ball), stinkbait, cheese, meat and bread; cut bait including chunks of smelt, carp and herring; natural bait including crayfish, shrimp, worms, leeches, grasshoppers and crickets

Life span: about 11 years

IGFA World Record: 123 lbs. 9 oz., Ken Paulie, Elk City Reservoir, Independence, Kansas, USA, May 14, 1998

DID YOU KNOW? The Flathead Catfish has a reputation as an outstanding sport fish. Catfish can be as small as your fingernail or as big as a nurse shark. Some catfish are transparent; they have the best camouflage of all. Catfish eggs are large and stick together in a glob like a fat pancake. Since they are all stuck together, the parents need to fan the eggs with their fins so they get enough oxygen.

 natural **processed**

CATFISH, FLATHEAD
Pylodictis olivaris

Common Names: mud cat, yellow cat, shovelnose and pied cat

Size: 3-15 lbs.; up to 35" in length

Habitat: rivers and reservoirs

Range: upper Midwest including the Mississippi River Valley, Missouri and Ohio River Basins and the Great Lakes south to the Gulf

Food: insects, crustaceans (e.g. crayfish), mollusks (e.g. clams) and fish

Mating: each spring the male and female construct a nest usually in heavy cover; the female lays hundreds to thousands of eggs; the male fertilizes the eggs and guards the nest and young

Description: brown in color with mottled yellow sides and whitish undersides; squared tail and several barbels (whiskers)

Bait: processed baits including doughballs (made from ingredients such as cornmeal or cornflakes and syrup and rolled into a ball), stinkbait, cheese, meat and bread; cut bait including chunks of smelt, carp and herring; natural bait including crayfish, shrimp, worms, leeches, grasshoppers and crickets

Life span: unknown

IGFA World Record: 4 lbs. 8 oz., L. Carl Herring, Jr., Ker Lake, Virginia, USA, Mar. 1, 1981

DID YOU KNOW? One of the larger panfish, the Black Crappie is highly prized by anglers for its tasty meat. Although it naturally feeds during morning and evening hours, it is reported that night fishing for this species is sometimes successful; the lights on boats and docks attract minnows which in turn attract crappies. Although difficult to know from its spelling, the correct pronunciation of its name is "croppie."

 natural **artificial**

CRAPPIE, BLACK
Pomoxis nigromaculatus

Common Names: speckled perch, grass bass, paper-mouth, shiner and speckled bass

Size: usually less than 2 lbs.; up to 13" in length

Habitat: lakes, ponds, sloughs, creeks, streams and backwaters

Range: widely distributed throughout the U.S.

Food: crustaceans (e.g. crayfish), insects and small fish; most active early in the morning

Mating: late each spring the male creates a nest within a nesting colony, the female lays thousands of eggs; the male fertilizes the eggs; the young hatch in 3-5 days

Description: greenish to bronze in color with dark, irregular blotches

Bait: natural bait including minnows, grasshoppers, crickets, grubs, mealworms and worms; various lures including small spinnerbait, plastic grubs and jigs

Life span: unknown

IGFA World Record: 5 lbs. 3 oz., Fred L. Bright, Enid Dam Mississippi, USA, July 31, 1957

DID YOU KNOW? The White Crappie can be distinguishe from its relative, the Black Crappie, by counting the numbe of spines on its first dorsal fin. The White Crappie has 6 spine while the Black Crappie has 7-8 spines. The White Crappi forms large schools and can survive in water with tempera tures approaching 85 degrees Fahrenheit. The White Crappi is the state fish of Louisiana.

 natural artificial

CRAPPIE, WHITE
Pomoxis annularis

Common Names: papermouth, speckled perch, bachelor perch, silver bass and calico bass

Size: usually less than 2 lbs.; up to 15" in length

Habitat: lakes and rivers

Range: widely distributed throughout U.S.

Food: small fish, fish eggs and insects

Mating: early each spring or summer the male creates a nest within a nesting colony; the female lays 27,000-68,000 eggs; the male fertilizes the eggs; the male guards the eggs and young which develop in 2-4 days

Description: light green to silver with purple shadowing and spots arranged in 7-9 vertical bars

Bait: natural bait including minnows, grasshoppers and worms; various lures including small spinnerbait, plastic grubs and jigs

Life span: about 8 years

IGFA World Record: 94 lbs. 2 oz.; David G. Deuel, Avon, North Carolina, USA, Nov. 7, 1984

DID YOU KNOW? The Red Drum makes a loud drumming sound to attract a mate. The drumming sound is created when the fish contracts a muscle that smacks against its swim bladder. Fish can hear each other over great distances because sound carries better underwater than through air. The Red Drum, commonly referred to as "channel bass," is the state fish of North Carolina.

 natural artificial

DRUM, RED
Sciaenops ocellatus

mmon Names: channel bass, redfish, spot-tail bass, red bass, red dorse, school drum and puppy drum

Size: 3-25 lbs.; up to 35" in length

Habitat: coastal estuaries, bays, inlets and channels

Range: Atlantic and Gulf coasts

Food: crustaceans (e.g. shrimp, crabs and sand dollars) and fish

Mating: late each summer or early fall males and females make a loud drumming sound as they pursue a mate; females release millions of eggs and males fertilize them

scription: copper red in color with silver undersides and one or more black spots on the tail, which is squared; the male changes color during mating becoming bright red or blue-gray

Bait: natural baits including crab and shrimp; various lures including spoons, surface plugs and jigs

Life span: about 50 years

IGFA World Record: 67 lbs. 8 oz., Cal Johnson, Lake Cour Oreilles, Hayward, Wisconsin, USA, July 24, 1949

DID YOU KNOW? A North American original, the Muskellunge is one of the largest freshwater fish. Nicknamed "fish of a thousand casts," it has the reputation of being notoriously difficult to catch. It may ignore lures passing right in front of its eyes or it may follow a lure right to the boat several times, only to quickly turn and dart away. When it does strike, it bites hard, adding to the angler's excitement. Some musky lures are as long as 14". The Muskellunge is the state fish of Wisconsin.

artificial

MUSKELLUNGE
Esox masquinongy

Common Names: muskie, lunge, maskinonge and great pike

Size: 7-30 lbs.; up to 51" in length

Habitat: streams, rivers and lakes

Range: central U.S., east including Great Lakes and Mississippi River Valley; widely stocked

Food: fish, amphibians (frogs and salamanders), crustaceans (e.g. crayfish), ducklings, mice and muskrats

Mating: early each spring the male and female form mating pairs; the fertilized eggs are randomly scattered; the young hatch within 8-14 days

Description: color varies, includes brown or green with numerous dark vertical bars or spots

Bait: various lures including large jigs, diving plugs, surface plugs, jerkbaits, crankbaits and buzzbaits

Life span: about 30 years

IGFA World Record: 4 lbs. 12 oz., Earl Small, Messalonskee Lake, Maine, USA, June 4, 1949

DID YOU KNOW? Unlike some fish that find food by smell (e.g. catfish), perch find food by sight. They can't see well in dim light so they typically feed during the day, resting on the bottom at night. Actually a member of the bass family, the White Perch is totally indiscriminate in terms of the prey it eats, even feeding on its own young.

 natural artificial

PERCH, WHITE
Morone americana

Common Names: silver bass, sea perch, humpy and gray perch

Size: average 4-12 oz. seldom exceeds 2 lbs.; up to 9" in length

Habitat: saltwater including estuaries, coastal streams and bays; freshwater ponds and lakes

Range: widely distributed along the Atlantic coast, Great Lakes and Chesapeake Bay

Food: insects, small fish and crustaceans (e.g. crabs and shrimp)

Mating: each spring the female lays 15,000-200,000 eggs; the male fertilizes the eggs; the young hatch in 1-4 days

Description: color varies, includes olive, grayish green, dark brown or black with lighter undersides

Bait: natural baits including small minnows and worms; various lures including small spinners, diving plugs and jigs

Life span: about 5-7 years

IGFA World Record: 4 lbs. 3 oz., Dr. C. C. Abbot, Bordentown New Jersey, USA, May, 1865

DID YOU KNOW? The Yellow Perch lays eggs in long, sticky bands that cling to rocks and other structures. These ribbon-like bands can measure a few inches wide by several feet long. Hatching in huge numbers, many of the small fry become meals for larger fish such as walleye and pike. Yellow Perch swim in large schools of 50-200 fish, which provide protection by visually confusing predators. They rely heavily on the concealment of cover including submerged trees, bridges and sunken boats. They may even take cover under a fishing boat!

 natural **artificial**

PERCH, YELLOW
Perca flavescens

mon Names: ringed perch, striped perch, jack perch and lake perch

Size: usually less than one pound; up to 16" in length

Habitat: lakes, ponds and rivers

Range: northern U.S. and Great Lakes states, sparse numbers in the west and south; heavily stocked

Food: fish, fish eggs, insects and crustaceans (e.g. crayfish)

Mating: early each spring the female lays 10,000-48,000 eggs that are fertilized by multiple males; young hatch within 10-21 days

scription: golden yellow in color with lighter undersides and 6-8 dark wide vertical bars; orange fins

Bait: natural bait including worms, minnows, mealworms, crawlers and grubs; various lures including jigs and spinners

Life span: up to 12 years

IGFA World Record: 9 lbs. 6 oz., Baxley McQuaig, Jr Homerville, Georgia, USA, Feb. 17, 1961

DID YOU KNOW? The Chain Pickerel is a vicious predato that relies heavily on its sense of sight to hunt and catch it prey. It also relies on the element of surprise ambushing it prey at breakneck speeds. Commonly referred to as "wate wolf," it uses its powerful jaws and long sharp teeth to kill it prey, sometimes swallowing it whole.

  natural artificial

PICKEREL, CHAIN
Esox niger

Common Names: grass pike, duck-billed pike, jack, river pike and lake pickerel

Size: average 1-3 lbs.; up to 30" in length

Habitat: lakes, ponds, swamps, rivers, streams and reservoirs

Range: eastern Atlantic states south to Florida and the Gulf west to Mississippi River Valley and Missouri River Valley

Food: fish, amphibians (frogs and salamanders), insects and crustaceans (e.g. crayfish)

Mating: early each spring the female lays up to 50,000 eggs; the male fertilizes the eggs; young hatch within 14 days

Description: olive green in color with dark, chain-like markings, yellowish undersides and dark vertical bar under each eye

Bait: natural bait including minnows and worms; various lures including minnow-plugs, spinnerbait with colorful blades, spoons and jigs

Life span: about 4 years

NFWFHF Record: 46 lbs. 2 oz., Peter Dubuc, Sacandaga Reservoir, New York, NY, USA, Sept. 15, 1940

DID YOU KNOW? Many northern anglers pursue the Northern Pike during the frigid months of winter by fishing through the ice. Ice fishing is a huge sport, which involves cutting a hole in the ice of a frozen lake, usually with an auger or chainsaw. Some anglers build shack-like structures called ice fishing houses. In fact, entire towns of ice-fishing houses are constructed on large lakes throughout the north including Lake Mille Lacs in central Minnesota, where up to 7,000 ice fishing houses are erected each year. The Northern Pike is highly prized by anglers and is the state fish of North Dakota.

 artificial

PIKE, NORTHERN
Esox lucius

mmon Names: great northern pike, jack, jackfish, pickerel, snake and gator

Size: 2-7 lbs.; up to 30" in length

Habitat: lakes, ponds and rivers

Range: north, Midwest and Great Lakes states; widely introduced in the south and west

Food: fish, amphibians (frogs and salamanders), crustaceans (e.g. crayfish), mice, muskrats and ducklings

Mating: early each spring, the female scatters thousands of eggs that are later fertilized; the young hatch within 12-14 days

scription: color varies, includes silver, blue or olive green with golden horizontal streaks, spots or bars

Bait: various large, brightly colored lures including red and white spoons, jigs, spinnerbait, deep-diving plugs, crankbait and plastic worms

Life span: about 7-10 years

IGFA World Record: No North American IGFA World Record or NFWFHF Record available. Certified State Record 116 lbs. 10 oz., John Hessler, Boca Raton, Florida, USA, May 5, 1996

DID YOU KNOW? A member of the billfish family, the Atlantic Sailfish is well known for its aerial gymnastics and speed. It can swim up to 68 mph over short distances. The Atlantic Sailfish has some of the largest vertebrae of all bony fishes. Their size allows the sailfish to swim as fast as it does. The Atlantic Sailfish represents a real challenge to many sport fish anglers due to its long, sword-like bill, tremendous speed and jumping ability and imposing size. It may weigh upwards of 100 pounds and exceed ten feet in length. The Atlantic Sailfish is the saltwater state fish of Florida.

 natural artificial

SAILFISH, ATLANTIC
Istiophorus platypterus

mmon Names: sailfish, sail, spikefish, spindlebeak, spindlesnoot and mylmeen

Size: average 20-100 lbs.; up to 84" in length

Habitat: warm, offshore saltwater

Range: Atlantic and Pacific

Food: fish and invertebrates (e.g. squid and octopus)

Mating: each summer the female lays over 4 million eggs; the male fertilizes the eggs, which develop quickly; young can grow up to 5' in the first year

scription: dark blue in color with a bluish brown midsection and silvery white undersides; long bill and prominent blue dorsal fin with dark spots

Bait: natural bait including fish; various lures including off-shore trolling lures and spoons

Life span: about 10 years

NFWFHF Record: 22 lbs. 11 oz., Frank J. McGrath Lobstick Lake, Newfoundland, Canada, Aug. 24, 1982

DID YOU KNOW? The anadromous Atlantic Salmon spend its early life in large rivers, then migrates to the sea where it grows quickly. Before returning to the river to spawn, it can travel great distances. Some Atlantic Salmon marked in Europe were later found in Greenland! It is the second larges salmon species. Unlike the Pacific salmon, the Atlantic Salmon can spawn more than once. The Atlantic Salmon is the state fish of Maine.

This species is threatened or endangered in all or part of it range. Please contact your local fish and wildlife office for fish ing regulations.

 natural **artificial**

SALMON, ATLANTIC
Salmo salar

mmon Names: landlocked salmon, grilt, fiddler, grayling, ouananiche and sebago salmon

Size: 5-10 lbs.; up to 23" in length

Habitat: lakes and rivers (landlocked species); freshwater and saltwater (anadromous species)

Range: Great Lakes and lakes and rivers of northeastern U.S. (landlocked species); coastal waters of northeastern U.S., especially Maine (anadromous species); widely introduced

Food: small fish, crustaceans (e.g. shrimp) and insects

Mating: the landlocked Atlantic Salmon moves into tributaries to mate; the anadromous Atlantic Salmon migrates from saltwater to freshwater streams to mate; each fall the female creates a large redd (nest-like depression); and lays thousands of eggs; the male fertilizes the eggs; the young develop slowly at 100+ days

scription: color varies, includes yellowish brown, blackish, dark blue or gray in color with red splotches and lighter undersides and dark X-shaped markings; the jaws of spawning males become elongated

Bait: natural bait including worms, crayfish tails and fish eggs; various lures including flies, spoons and plugs

Life span: about 8 years

IGFA World Record: 97 lbs. 4 oz., Les Anderson, Kena
River, Alaska, USA, May 17, 1985

DID YOU KNOW? Scientists have monitored its amazing
spawning migration using radio-tracking tags that are
attached to a fin. Individual fish have swum over 2,000 miles
from the Pacific Ocean to the freshwater streams where it was
hatched in just 60 days. Mature Chinook Salmon have black
coloring inside their mouths. The largest member of the
salmon family, the Chinook Salmon is the state fish of Oregon
and Alaska where it is commonly called King Salmon.

*This species is threatened or endangered in all or part of its
range. Please contact your local fish and wildlife office for
fishing regulations.*

 natural artificial

SALMON, CHINOOK
Oncorhynchus tshawytscha

Common Names: king salmon, spring salmon, tyee, quinnat, blackmouth and blackjaw

Size: average 15-30 lbs.; up to 46" in length

Habitat: saltwater and freshwater

Range: Pacific Ocean from southern California north to Alaska; stocked in Atlantic, Gulf and inland lakes including Great Lakes

Food: insects, fish, crustaceans (e.g. shrimp and crab) and invertebrates (e.g. squid)

Mating: an anadromous species (migrates from saltwater to freshwater to spawn); some migrate as far as 1,500-2,000 miles without eating; the female digs a large redd (nest-like depression) and lays 3,000-14,000 eggs; upon hatching, the young spend up to a year in freshwater before migrating to saltwater

Description: bluish to gray in color with silver undersides and dark spots on back and tail; spawning (mating) fish vary in color including red, copper, brown and black; during spawning the males develop a hooked snout called a kype

Bait: natural bait including worms, crayfish tails and fish eggs; various lures including flies, spoons, plugs and spinners

Life span: unknown

IGFA World Record: 33 lbs. 4 oz., Jerry Lifton, Salmon River, Pulaski, New York, USA, Sept. 27, 1989

DID YOU KNOW? Anglers prize the Coho Salmon as a strong, aerial fighter. Amazingly, it has been known to travel up to 1,200 miles from the Pacific Ocean to the freshwater stream where it originally hatched. Like most Pacific Salmon, the Coho Salmon does not eat during the spawning migration, causing its condition to deteriorate drastically. It dies soon after spawning.

This species is threatened or endangered in all or part of its range. Please contact your local fish and wildlife office for fishing regulations.

 natural **artificial**

SALMON, COHO
Oncorhynchus kisutch

Common Names: sea trout, silver salmon, blueback, hookbill and hooknose

Size: average 4-12 lbs.; up to 30" in length

Habitat: saltwater and freshwater

Range: Pacific Ocean from southern California north to Alaska; stocked in Atlantic, Gulf and inland lakes including Great Lakes

Food: insects, fish, invertebrates (e.g. squid) and crustaceans

Mating: an anadromous species (migrates from saltwater to freshwater to spawn); spawning onset varies with location; female digs a large redd (nest-like depression) and lays 1,500-4,500 eggs; male fertilizes the eggs; upon hatching, young spend up to a year in freshwater before migrating to saltwater

Description: color varies, includes dark blue to blue-green in color with black spots and silver undersides; during spawning the males develop a hooked snout called a kype and turn green with red sides and black undersides; the female's undersides turn pinkish red

Bait: natural bait including worms, crayfish tails and fish eggs; various lures including flies, spoons, plugs and spinners

Life-span: unknown

IGFA World Record: 15 lbs. 3 oz., Stan Roach, Kenai River, Alaska, USA, Aug. 9, 1987

DID YOU KNOW? The salmons' sense of smell helps them navigate the rivers to find their spawning grounds. In an experiment, salmon whose smell was blocked often went up the wrong fork of the river they had traveled down. Those with unblocked smell consistently found their way back.

This species is threatened or endangered in all or part of its range. Please contact your local fish and wildlife office for fishing regulations.

 natural **artificial**

SALMON, SOCKEYE
Oncorhynchus nerka

Common Names: red salmon, blueback salmon and kokanee salmon (landlocked form)

Size: 4-8 lbs.; up to 33" in length

Habitat: saltwater and freshwater

Range: Pacific Northwest, Alaska; introduced elsewhere in the west

Food: crustaceans (e.g. shrimp), fish, invertebrates (e.g. squid) and insects

Mating: an anadromous species (migrates from saltwater to freshwater to spawn); some travel thousands of miles without eating between July and February; the female digs a large redd (nest-like depression) and lays 2,000-4,500 eggs; the male and female die soon after spawning; upon hatching, the young spend up to 3 years in freshwater before migrating to saltwater

Description: greenish to blue in color with lighter, silvery undersides; spawning fish change color becoming dark red with a greenish head; spawning males develop a humped back and elongated jaws

Bait: natural bait including worms; various lures including plugs, spinners, small spoons and flies

Life span: about 5 years

IGFA World Record: 8 lbs. 12 oz., Mike Fischer, Lake Sakakawea, North Dakota, USA, Oct. 6, 1971

DID YOU KNOW? A member of the perch family and a close relative to the Walleye, the slightly smaller Sauger has better vision in turbid water and darkness, an important factor in its habitat. While they look quite a lot alike, look for the rows of black spots on the dorsal fin of the sauger, and the white tip on the lower part of the tail of the walleye.

 natural artificial

SAUGER
Stizostedion canadense

Common Names: gray pike, river pike, jack, jackfish and sandpickerel

Size: 1-2 lbs.; up to 15" in length

Habitat: lakes and rivers; can live in murky or turbid waters

Range: mid-central Atlantic states west to Montana and south to Texas; widely stocked

Food: fish, crayfish and insects

Mating: each spring spawning activity begins as the males and females travel to backwaters or tributaries; the female lays hundreds to thousands of eggs; the male fertilizes the eggs

Description: color varies, includes brown or olive with mottled rusty-black blotches

Bait: natural baits including worms and minnows; various lures including spinners, spoons, jigs, plugs and flies

Life span: about 10-12 years

IGFA World Record: 2 lbs. 2 oz., Paul M. Dilley, Stockton Lake, Missouri, USA, June 18, 1971

DID YOU KNOW? The Green Sunfish is more tolerant of turbid water and drought conditions than other members of the sunfish family. Females are not choosy about where they deposit their eggs and may do so in nests made by males that are not even Green Sunfish. Unlike some other fish that need large areas for breeding, the sunfish breed close to each other. Green sunfish may hybridize with Pumpkinseed Sunfish or Bluegills, making identification even more complicated.

natural

SUNFISH, GREEN
Lepomis cyanellus

mmon Names: green perch, black perch, blue-spotted sunfish, sand bass and creek perch

Size: average less than ½ lb.; up to 12" in length

Habitat: streams, backwaters, ponds and lakes

Range: northeast, Mississippi River Valley and Great Lakes to Gulf

Food: insects, crustaceans (e.g. shrimp) and small fish

Mating: spawning from April through August; the male builds a saucer-shaped nest usually near rocks or logs; the female lays eggs; multiple males may fertilize the eggs; young hatch within 3-5 days

scription: color varies, includes brown, olive or blue green with bluish spots, lighter undersides, variable dark bars and prominent gill cover

Bait: natural bait including meal worms, worms, wax worms, crickets, grasshoppers and shrimp

Life-span: unknown

IGFA World Record: 1 lb. 12 oz., Patricia Stout, Elephan Butte Lake, New Mexico, USA, May 9, 1985

DID YOU KNOW? A very colorful fish, the Longear Sunfish i popular with aquarium enthusiasts and anglers alike. This sun fish gets its name from the Greek words *Lepomis* (scaled g cover) and *megalotis* (great ear).

 natural

SUNFISH, LONGEAR

Lepomis megalotis

mmon Names: longear

Size: average less than ½ lb.; up to 9½" in length

Habitat: lakes, ponds, rivers, streams, creeks and reservoirs

Range: throughout much of the U.S.

Food: insects, worms, crustaceans (e.g. crayfish) and fish eggs

Mating: spawning from May to August; the male creates a saucer-shaped nest; the female lays up to several thousand eggs; the male fertilizes the eggs and guards them until they develop, usually 5-7 days

scription: color varies, includes red with blue spots and yellow-orange undersides, red eyes and black earflap edged with white

Bait: natural bait including meal worms, worms, wax worms, crickets, grasshoppers and shrimp

Life-span: unknown

NFWFHF Record: 2 lbs. 4 oz., Scott Hart, North Saluda River, South Carolina, USA, May 26, 1997

DID YOU KNOW? The name pumpkinseed is derived from the shape of the fish. While it looks similar to the bluegill, note the orange spot near the gill. Pumpkinseeds, Green Sunfish and Bluegills can often be found nesting together. The Pumpkinseed Sunfish is readily caught by young anglers.

 natural artificial

SUNFISH, PUMPKINSEED
Lepomis gibbosus

mmon Names: yellow sunfish, speckled perch, bream and sunny

Size: average less than 1 lb.; up to 9" in length

Habitat: lakes, ponds, rivers and creeks

Range: throughout the Midwest east to the Atlantic and south to the Gulf; widely stocked

Food: insects, mollusks (e.g. snails) and fish

Mating: each spring the male creates a nest generally near the shoreline; the female lays hundreds to thousands of eggs; the eggs hatch in 3 days; the male guards the young for a short period

scription: color varies, includes orange or olive with blue markings and a black earflap with red spot

Bait: natural bait including worms, minnows and grubs; various lures including jigs, spinners, crankbait and flies

Life span: about 10 years

IGFA World Record: 5 lbs. 7 oz., Amos M. Gay, Diversor Canal, Georgia, USA, Nov. 6, 1998

DID YOU KNOW? Sometimes called the shellcracker, the Redear Sunfish uses special molar-like teeth in its throat to break open snails, an important part of its diet.

 natural artificial

SUNFISH REDEAR
Lepomis microlophus

mmon Names: yellow bream, bream, shellcracker

Size: averages under ½ lb.; up to 9" in length

Habitat: ponds, swamps, lakes and rivers

Range: throughout the U.S.

Food: crustaceans (e.g. crayfish), insects and mollusks (e.g. snails and clams)

Mating: spawning activity occurs from spring to fall; the male builds a circular nest; the female lays thousands of eggs; the male fertilizes the eggs and guards them

scription: color varies, includes dark olive to golden with lighter undersides and a black earflap edged with reddish orange

Bait: natural bait including worms, wax worms, crickets, grasshoppers, minnows and grubs; various lures including jigs, spinners, crankbait and flies

Life span: about 8 years

IGFA World Record: No North American IGFA World Record or NFWFHF Record available. Certified State Record 243 lbs., Gus Bell, Key West, Florida, USA, February 17, 197?

DID YOU KNOW? Many anglers consider the Tarpon to be the ultimate sport fish due to its tremendous size and fighting ability. When the Tarpon can't get enough oxygen from the water, it will actually gulp air at the surface, which is referred to as rolling. It has some of the largest scales; each scale is more than two inches across. The Tarpon is the saltwater state fish of Alabama.

 natural artificial

TARPON, SILVER KING
Megalops atlanticus

nmon Names: silver king, silverfish and tarpum

Size: average 40-100 lbs.; up to 96" in length

Habitat: coastal waters, estuaries, lakes and rivers

Range: Atlantic and Gulf

Food: fish, crustaceans (e.g. crabs) and invertebrates (e.g. squid)

Mating: each spring the tarpon migrates to an off-shore spawning site; the female lays more than 20 million eggs; upon development, the young travel to still waters such as coastal swamps

scription: color varies, includes greenish blue with dark silvery sides; very large scales, upturned lower jaw and a deeply forked tail

Bait: natural bait including fish, crab and shrimp; various lures including plugs, flies, spoons and jigs

Life span: about 16 years

IGFA World Record: 5 lbs. 3 oz., John Baldwin, White Mtn., Apache Reservoir, Arizona, USA, May 29, 1991

DID YOU KNOW? Trout do not have any spiny fins; all of them are soft. The Apache Trout is one of the chunkiest of all trout and is one of only two trout native to Arizona. Competition from introduced trout species and inter-species mating has significantly reduced the Apache Trout population. The Apache Trout is the state fish of Arizona.

This species is threatened or endangered in all or part of its range. Please contact your local fish and wildlife office for fishing regulations.

 artificial

TROUT, APACHE
Oncorhynchus apache

Common Names: Arizona trout

Size: average less than 3 lbs.; up to 18" in length

Habitat: lakes and streams

Range: east central Arizona

Food: fish and insects

Mating: spawning activity varies from early spring to early summer; the female builds a redd (nest-like depression); the female lays 200-4,000 eggs; the male fertilizes the eggs

Description: golden with dark spots and copper colored head

Bait: various lures including flies, spoons, plugs, spinners and jigs

Life-span: unknown

IGFA World Record: No IGFA World Record available. No NFWFHF Record available.

DID YOU KNOW? Trout can see fishing line in the water and avoid it, so most trout anglers use very thin line. If a trout is spooked by noise or movement in its feeding area, it is very reluctant to continue eating and will hide. The Bonneville Cutthroat Trout is the state fish of Utah and one of 40 known species of trout found in North America.

While this fish is neither threatened nor endangered, it is listed as a sensitive species.

 artificial

TROUT, BONNEVILLE CUTTHROAT
Oncorhynchus clarkii utah

Common Names: native trout, Utah trout and bluehead

Size: 4-18 lbs.; up to 30" in length

Habitat: streams and lakes

Range: western states including Utah, Wyoming, Nevada and Idaho

Food: insects and fish

Mating: spawning activity varies from early spring to summer; the female digs a redd (nest-like depression); the female lays thousands of eggs; the male fertilizes the eggs

Description: yellowish in color with uniform spotting and reddish orange slash marks on the throat

Bait: various lures including flies, jigs, spoons, spinners and plugs

Life span: about 20 years

IGFA World Record: 14 lbs. 8 oz., W. J. Cook, Nipigon River Ontario, Canada, July, 1916

DID YOU KNOW? Brook Trout can eat, digest and be rid of their food in less than 20 minutes. In cold water, Brook Trout eggs can take up to 144 days to hatch; in warm water, eggs hatch in about 35 days. Similar in appearance to other trout as well as salmon, the Brook Trout is actually a Char which is characterized by having light markings on a dark background, whereas trout have dark markings on a light background. Native to North America, the Brook Trout is the state fish of Michigan, New Jersey, New York, Pennsylvania, Virginia and West Virginia, and the freshwater state fish of New Hampshire.

 artificial

TROUT, BROOK
Salvelinus fontinalis

Common Names: eastern brook trout, brookie, coaster, salter, speckled trout, native trout and squaretail

Size: average less than 3 lbs.; up to 18" in length

Habitat: primarily a freshwater species, though some live in saltwater

Range: across much of the northeast south to Georgia and west to the Mississippi River Valley; widely stocked

Food: insects, fish, crustaceans (e.g. crayfish), mice and snakes

Mating: an anadromous species (migrates from saltwater to freshwater to spawn); however, many Brook Trout dwell exclusively in freshwater; late each fall the female digs several redds (nest-like depressions); and lays hundreds to thousands of eggs; the male fertilizes the eggs; the young usually develop within 80 days

Description: color varies, includes dark olive, gray, blue or brown with vermiculations (light, worm-like markings); large pale spots and small red spots ringed with blue

Bait: various lures including flies, jigs, spoons, spinners and plugs

Life span: about 15 years

IGFA World Record: 40 lbs. 4 oz., Howard L. (Rip) Collins, Little Red River, Heber Springs, Arkansas, USA, May 9, 1992

DID YOU KNOW? When trout are young, they eat mostly insects and crustaceans; as they get older, they eat more fish. A popular sport fish in Europe, the Brown Trout was first introduced into the U.S. in 1884 at Michigan's Pere Marquette River. A wary and difficult fish to catch, the Brown Trout grows faster than other trout species and is often stocked in streams with heavy fishing pressure.

 natural  **processed** **artificial**

TROUT, BROWN
Salmo trutta

mmon Names: brownie, river trout, brook trout and lake trout

Size: 1-5 lbs.; 9-14" in length

Habitat: rivers and lakes

Range: throughout central, western and northern U.S.; widely introduced

Food: insects, fish, crustaceans (e.g. crayfish), mollusks (e.g. snails) and amphibians (e.g. frogs and salamanders)

Mating: spawning activity varies from October to February; adults migrate to rivers or lake tributaries; the female excavates a nest and lays 200-5,000 eggs; the male fertilizes the eggs; the female covers the eggs with bits of gravel

scription: varies in appearance depending on location; generally olive brown to silver in color with lighter undersides, many with red spots that are circled by light blue rings

Bait: natural bait including crayfish, worms and fish eggs; processed bait including cheese and corn; various lures including flies, jigs, plugs, spoons, spinners and crankbait

Life span: about 12 years

IGFA World Record: 41 lbs. 0 oz., John Skimmerhorn Pyramid Lake, Nevada, USA, Dec. 1925

DID YOU KNOW? The Cutthroat Trout is named for the bright, colorful slash mark under its lower jaw. It is also named for Captain William Clark, of Lewis and Clark fame, as indicated by its scientific name *Oncorhynchus clarkii*. Captain Clark wrote about the Cutthroat Trout while on his historical western expedition from the upper Missouri River to the Pacific Ocean in the early 1800s. The Cutthroat Trout is the state fish of Idaho, Montana and Wyoming.

 artificial

TROUT, CUTTHROAT
Oncorhynchus clarkii

Common Names: Clark's trout, native trout, cut, red-throat, mountain trout, black-spotted trout

Size: average 2-3 lbs.; up to 24" in length

Habitat: streams and lakes

Range: western U.S. including Alaska; introduced elsewhere

Food: insects, small fish, trout eggs, crustaceans (e.g. crayfish and shrimp) and amphibians (frogs and salamanders)

Mating: an anadromous species (migrates from saltwater to freshwater to spawn); however, many Cutthroat Trout dwell exclusively in freshwater; the female creates a redd (nest-like depression); and lays hundreds to thousands of eggs; the male fertilizes the eggs; the young hatch within 7 weeks; young anadromous fish remain in freshwater for several years before migrating to saltwater where they reach maturity

Description: color varies, includes blue, silver, olive or yellow with dark, black spots and prominent orange-red slash-like markings under lower jaw

Bait: various lures including flies, spinners, spoons and plugs

Life span: about 7 years

IGFA World Record: 11 lbs. 0 oz., Chas S. Reed, Cook Lake, Wyoming, USA, Aug. 5, 1948

DID YOU KNOW? Trout have very good eyesight and ca see the outlines of anglers through the water when they loo up. Trout eat during times when the light is dim, such a mornings or evenings or on overcast days. Big trout will ea first, then the smaller trout. The Golden Trout is the freshwa ter state fish of California.

 artificial

TROUT, GOLDEN
Oncorhynchus aguabonita

mmon Names: Kern River trout, mountain trout and goldie

Size: average 1-4 lbs.; up to 14" in length

Habitat: lakes and streams at altitudes above 6,000 feet; stocked at lower elevations

Range: California; introduced in Washington, Idaho and Wyoming

Food: insects and crustaceans (e.g. crayfish)

Mating: each summer the female digs several redds (nest-like depressions) and lays hundreds to thousands of eggs; the male fertilizes the eggs

scription: varies in color depending on altitude; generally dark olive with golden sides, reddish orange undersides and cheeks, a reddish horizontal band with 10 dark ovals (called parr marks) and dark spots

Bait: various lures including flies, spinners, spoons and plugs

Life span: about 7 years

IGFA World Record: No IGFA World Record available. N
NFWFHF Record available.

DID YOU KNOW? Highly prized by anglers across the wes
all trout are admired for their brilliant color and hard-fightin
character. The fishing can be fast and furious. In fact, in 1974
a Yellowstone Park Ranger caught and released 133 fish i
just two hours! The Greenback Cutthroat Trout is the state fis
of Colorado.

*This species is threatened or endangered in all or part of it
range. Please contact your local fish and wildlife office fc
fishing regulations.*

artificial

TROUT, GREENBACK CUTTHROAT

Oncorhynchus clarkii stomias

mmon Names: none

Size: average 2-3 lbs.; up to 18" in length

Habitat: freshwater lakes and rivers

Range: Colorado and Wyoming

Food: insects and fish

Mating: each spring the female digs a large redd (nest-like depression) and lays hundreds to thousands of eggs; the male fertilizes the eggs

scription: greenish in color with large spots (called parr marks) and bright red slash marks on gill covering

Bait: various lures including flies, spinners, spoons and plugs

Life span: about 7 years

IGFA World Record: No IGFA World Record or NFWFHF Record available. Certified State Record: 41 lbs., Pyramid Lake, Nevada, USA, 1925.

DID YOU KNOW? Trout are spooked by thunderstorms and anglers might not have much luck catching them for a day or two after a severe storm. The Lahontan Cutthroat Trout is the largest of the 14 subspecies of cutthroat trout. Like all trout species, the Lahontan Cutthroat Trout has no stiff spines in its fins. Instead, they are soft to the touch. The Lahontan Cutthroat Trout is the state fish of Nevada.

This species is threatened or endangered in all or part of its range. Please contact your local fish and wildlife office for fishing regulations.

artificial

TROUT, LAHONTAN CUTTHROAT
Oncorhynchus clarkii henshawi

Common Names: native trout

Size: up to 5 lbs.; up to 25" in length

Habitat: lakes, streams and rivers

Range: California and Nevada; widely stocked

Food: insects and fish

Mating: each spring the female builds a redd (nest-like depression); the female lays hundreds to thousands of eggs; the male fertilizes the eggs

Description: golden-bronze in color with lighter undersides, dark spots and reddish orange slash marks around throat

Bait: various lures including flies, spinners, spoons and plugs

Life-span: unknown

IGFA World Record: 72 lbs. 0 oz., Lloyd E. Bull, Great Bear Lake, N.W.T., Canada, Aug. 19, 1995

DID YOU KNOW? During the warmer months, Lake Trout will swim 200 feet underwater to find the cold water in which they are most comfortable. In the early 1900s, the Lake Trout was one of the most important commercial fish in the Great Lakes. By the 1940s, however, the Lake Trout population had collapsed due to excessive predation by sea lampreys and overfishing. The population in the Great Lakes has begun to rebound, thanks to control of the lamprey population and con- tinuous stocking.

 artificial

TROUT, LAKE
Salvelinus namaycush

Common Names: landlocked salmon, bank trout, bumper, paperbelly, gray trout and laker

Size: average 2-11 lbs.; up to 48" in length

Habitat: lakes and rivers

Range: northwest from Alaska, across the Great Lakes and east to New England; heavily stocked

Food: insects, crustaceans (e.g. crayfish), mollusks (e.g. clams and snails) and fish

Mating: early each fall spawning activity begins; the female releases hundreds to thousands of eggs; the eggs do not hatch until the following spring because the water temperature is very cold

Description: color varies, includes green, gray, brown or black with light, irregular spots and forked tail

Bait: various lures including spoons, spinners and flies

Life span: about 20 years

IGFA World Record: 42 lbs. 2 oz., David Robert, White Bel Island, Alaska, USA, June 22, 1970

DID YOU KNOW? Trout have a good sense of smell. Migrating trout will retreat downstream when a bear or human comes in contact with the water. Trout can see most of the same colors we can. A very popular sport fish, the colorful Rainbow Trout it is highly prized by anglers worldwide for its hard-fighting character. It is one of the most widely distributed freshwater fish. The Rainbow Trout has been stocked in Europe, India, Australia, Africa and South America and is the only trout in Europe that has a spotted tail.

artificial

TROUT, RAINBOW
Oncorhynchus mykiss

Common Names: steelhead, rainbow, redband trout and redsides

Size: average 2-20 lbs.; up to 35" in length

Habitat: saltwater and freshwater

Range: Pacific Northwest; widely introduced elsewhere

Food: insects, crustaceans (e.g. crayfish), mollusks (e.g. snails) and fish

Mating: an anadromous species (migrates from saltwater to freshwater to spawn); however, many Rainbow Trout dwell exclusively in freshwater; early each spring the female creates a redd (nest-like depression) and lays 200-8,000 eggs; the male fertilizes the eggs and covers them with small bits of gravel until they develop

Description: color varies, includes steel-blue to slate with a broad pink or red lateral stripe, dark spots and lighter undersides

Bait: various lures including flies, jigs, spoons, spinners and plugs

Life span: about 4-6 years

IGFA World Record: No IGFA World Record available. No NFWFHF Record available.

DID YOU KNOW? Trout prefer to live in water that gets no warmer than 60 degrees Fahrenheit and will seek out deeper waters when the weather gets warmer. Trout have a highly sensitive lateral line; they can even feel the vibrations caused by people walking on streambanks. In 1541, Spanish explorers wrote of the excellent trout of New Mexico. The Rio Grande Cutthroat Trout is the southernmost species of cutthroat trout in the U.S. and is the state fish of New Mexico.

Please contact your local fish and wildlife office for the fishing rules that apply to this species.

 artificial

TROUT, RIO GRANDE CUTTHROAT
Oncorhynchus clarkii virginalis

mmon Names: New Mexico cutthroat trout

Size: average less than 1 lb.; up to 10" in length

Habitat: streams and rivers

Range: New Mexico

Food: insects and crustaceans (e.g. crayfish)

Mating: each spring the female lays 200-4,500 eggs; the male fertilizes the eggs

scription: color varies, includes yellowish green to grayish brown with scattered black spots; densely spotted tail

Bait: various lures including flies, jigs, spoons, spinners and plugs

Life span: about 8 years

IGFA World Record: No IGFA World Record available. No NFWFHF Record available.

DID YOU KNOW? Steelhead Trout are the fastest freshwater fish, swimming more than 25 feet in one second. It is the anadromous or saltwater form of the Rainbow Trout, which means it spends part of its life maturing in saltwater, and migrates to freshwater to spawn. Steelhead Trout do not die after spawning. The Steelhead Trout is the state fish of Washington.

This species is threatened or endangered in all or part of its range. Please contact your local fish and wildlife office for fishing regulations.

 artificial

TROUT, STEELHEAD
Oncorhynchus mykiss irideus

mmon Names: coastal rainbow trout, sea-run rainbow and steelies

Size: 5-12 lbs.; up to 35" in length

Habitat: saltwater and freshwater

Range: Pacific coast to Alaska; stocked in many areas including the Great Lakes

Food: crustaceans (e.g. shrimp), fish eggs and fish

Mating: an anadromous species (migrates from saltwater to freshwater to spawn); many migrate over 1,000 miles; however, some Steelhead Trout dwell exclusively in freshwater; each spring the female digs several redds (nest-like depressions) and lays hundreds to thousands of eggs in each redd; the male fertilizes the eggs; upon development, the young may remain in freshwater for several years

scription: color varies, includes steel-blue, slate or blue-green with black spots, a broad pinkish red lateral stripe and lighter undersides; color intensifies in spawning fish

Bait: various lures including flies, jigs, spoons, spinners and plugs

Life span: about 11 years

NFWFHF Record: 22 lbs. 11 oz., Al Nelson, Greer's Ferry Lake, Arkansas, USA, Mar. 14, 1982

DID YOU KNOW? The Walleye is the largest member of the perch family in the U.S. It is highly prized by anglers for its tasty meat. Often forming large schools, the Walleye's prominent, marble-like eyes provide it with tremendous night vision for hunting its prey. Walleyes can only see orange and green, other colors appear as shades of gray. The Walleye is the state fish of Minnesota, South Dakota and Vermont.

 natural artificial

WALLEYE
Stizostedion vitreum

Common Names: walleyed pike, green pike, pickerel and jackfish

Size: average 1-5 lbs.; up to 30" in length

Habitat: lakes, rivers and reservoirs

Range: Northeastern states south to the Carolinas and west through the Mississippi River Valley and Great Lakes; widely stocked

Food: fish, insects, crustaceans (e.g. crayfish) and mollusks (e.g. snails)

Mating: early each spring many males and females congregate to spawn (mate); the female randomly scatters hundreds of thousands of eggs; the young hatch within 12-18 days

Description: color varies, includes golden brown or dark green with lighter undersides and milky white, marble-like eyes

Bait: natural baits including minnows, crayfish, salamanders, night crawlers and leeches; various lures including jigs, plugs, spinners and spoons

Life span: about 26 years

IGFA World Record: 2 lbs. 7 oz., Tony David Dempsey, Guess Lake, Yellow River Holt, Florida, USA, Oct. 19, 1985

DID YOU KNOW? The Warmouth is a very popular panfish. Like most panfish, the Warmouth provides fast and furious fishing for young anglers as it generally travels in schools and is easily accessible in shallow water under docks and bridge pilings.

 natural artificial

WARMOUTH
Lepomis gulosus

Common Names: goggle-eye

Size: usually less than 1 lb.; up to 10" in length

Habitat: lakes, ponds, marshes, streams, creeks and reservoirs

Range: many eastern states, the Great Lakes and Mississippi River Valley south to the Gulf; widely stocked

Food: insects, fish, crustaceans (e.g. crayfish and shrimp) and mollusks (e.g. snails)

Mating: spawning activity occurs from early spring throughout the summer; often nest in colonies; the male creates a small, saucer-shaped nest; the female lays thousands of eggs; the male defends its nest by puffing out its gills and waving its tail at intruders

Description: olive-green in color with vertical barring and lighter undersides; three dark rays around the eyes; dark red spot on the earflap of spawning males

Bait: natural bait including worms, crickets and meal worms; various lures including small jigs and spinners

Life span: about 6-8 years

IGFA World Record: 19 lbs. 2 oz., William E. Thoma
Delaware Bay, Delaware, USA, May 20, 1989

DID YOU KNOW? A member of the drum family, th
Weakfish makes a loud drumming sound to attract a mat
The drumming sound is created when the fish contracts
muscle that smacks against its swim bladder. It is high
prized by anglers for its hard-hitting, fighting character ar
tender white meat. The Weakfish is named for its delica
mouth structure as membranes within its mouth are eas
torn when hooked. The Weakfish is the state fish of Delawar

 natural artificial

WEAKFISH
Cynoscion regalis

Common Names: tide runner, sea trout, yellow fin trout, yellow mouth, squeteague, gray trout and gray weakfish

Size: 1-6 lbs.; up to 36" in length

Habitat: saltwater marshes and estuaries

Range: Atlantic coast, especially around the mid-Atlantic states

Food: crustaceans (e.g. crabs and shrimp) and fish

Mating: spawning activity occurs from spring to early fall; the male makes a drumming sound to attract females; the female randomly lays thousands of eggs; the young hatch in 2 days

Description: olive to greenish blue in color with dark spots and coppery purple sides

Bait: natural baits including worms, shrimp, squid, small fish and eels; various lures including jigs, spoons and plugs

Life span: about 10 years

STATE FISH AND WILDLIFE AGENCIES

Alabama Division of Fish and Game
www.dcnr.state.al.us/agfd
(334) 242-3465

Alaska Department of Fish and Game
www.state.ak.us
(907) 465-4100

Arizona Game and Fish Department
www.gf.state.az.us
(602) 942-3000

Arkansas Game and Fish Commission
www.agfc.state.ar.us
(501) 223-6300

California Department of Fish and Game
www.dfg.ca.gov
(916) 653-7664

Colorado Division of Wildlife
www.wildlife.state.co.us
(303) 297-1192

Connecticut Department of Environmental Protection
www.dep.state.ct.us
(860) 424-3000

Delaware Division of Fish and Wildlife
www.dnrec.state.de.us
(302) 739-3441

District of Columbia Fisheries and Wildlife Division
www.dchealth.com/dcfishandwildlife
(202) 535-2260

rida Fish and Wildlife Conservation Commission
w.fcn.state.fl.us/gfc
0) 488-4676

orgia Dept of Nat Res/Wildlife Resources Division
w.dnr.state.ga.us
'0) 918-6406

waii Department of Land and Natural Resources
w.state.hi.us/dlnr
8) 587-0400

ho Fish and Game Department
w.state.id.us/fishgame
8) 334-3700

nois Department of Natural Resources
w.dnr.state.il.us
7) 782-6302

iana Department of Natural Resources
w.state.in.us/dnr/fishwild
7) 232-4200

va Department of Natural Resources
w.state.ia.us/government/dnr
5) 281-5918

nsas Department of Wildlife and Parks
w.kdwp.state.ks.us
0) 672-5911

ntucky Department of Fish and Wildlife Resources
w.kdfwr.state.ky.us
00-858-1549

Louisiana Department of Wildlife and Fisheries
www.wlf.state.la.us
(225) 765-2800

Maine Department of Inland Fisheries and Wildlife
www.state.me.us/ifw
(207) 287-8000

Maryland Department of Natural Resources
www.dnr.state.md.us
1-877-620-8DNR (8367)

Massachusetts Division of Fisheries and Wildlife
www.state.ma.us/dfwele/dfw
(508) 792-7270

Michigan Department of Natural Resources
www.dnr.state.mi.us
(517) 373-7540

Minnesota Department of Natural Resources
www.dnr.state.mn.us
(651) 296-6157 or 888-MINNDNR

Mississippi Department of Wildlife, Fisheries and Parks
www.mdwfp.com
(601) 432-2400

Missouri Department of Conservation
www.conservation.state.mo.us
(573) 751-4115

Montana Department of Fish, Wildlife and Parks
www.fwp.state.mt.us
(406) 444-2535

braska Game and Parks Commission
w.ngpc.state.ne.us/gp.
2) 471-0641

vada Dept of Conservation and Natural Resources
w.nevadadivisionofwildlife.org
5) 688-1500

w Hampshire Fish and Game Department
w.wildlife.state.nh.us
3) 271-3211

w Jersey Division of Fish and Wildlife
w.state.nj.us/dep/fgw
9) 292-2965

w Mexico Game and Fish Department
w.gmfsh.state.nm.us
5) 827-7911 or 1-800-862-9310

w York Department of Environmental Conservation
w.dec.state.ny.us
8) 457-5690 (Division of Fish and Wildlife)

rth Carolina Wildlife Resources Commission
w.wildlife.state.nc.us
9) 733-3391

rth Dakota Game and Fish Department
w.state.nd.us/gnf
1) 328-6300

io Division of Wildlife
w.dnr.state.oh.us/odnr/wildlife
4) 265-6565

Oklahoma Department of Wildlife Conservation
www.wildlifedepartment.com
(405) 521-3851

Oregon Department of Fish and Wildlife
www.dfw.state.or.us
(503) 872-5268

Pennsylvania Fish and Boat Commission
www.state.pa.us/PA_Exec/Fish_Boat
(717) 705-7800

Rhode Island Division of Fish and Wildlife
www.state.ri.us/dem/programs/bnatres/fishwild/index.htm
(401) 222-4700

South Carolina Department of Natural Resources
www.dnr.state.sc.us
(803) 734-3888

South Dakota Game Fish and Parks Department
www.state.sd.us/gfp
(605) 773-3485

Tennessee Wildlife Resources Agency
www.state.tn.us/twra
(615) 781-6500

Texas Parks and Wildlife Department
www.tpwd.state.tx.us
1-800-792-1112

Utah Division of Wildlife Resources
www.nr.state.ut.us/dwr/dwr.htm
(801) 538-4700

rmont Department of Fish and Wildlife
w.anr.state.vt.us/fw/fwhome
)2) 241-3700

ginia Department of Game and Inland Fisheries
w.dgif.state.va.us
)4) 367-1000

shington Department of Fish and Wildlife
w.wa.gov/wdfw
)0) 902-2200

st Virginia Division of Natural Resources
w.dnr.state.wv.us
)4) 558-2754

sconsin Department of Natural Resources
w.dnr.state.wi.us
)8) 266-2621

oming Game and Fish Department
w.gf.state.wy.us
)7) 777-4600

ATIONAL FISH AND WILDLIFE AGENCY

Fish and Wildlife Service
w.fws.gov

THER GAME FISH ORGANIZATIONS

ernational Game Fish Association (IGFA)
w.igfa.org
)4) 927-2628

tional Fresh Water Fishing Hall of Fame (NFWFHF)
w.Freshwater-Fishing.org
.5) 634-4440

CATCH LIST (RECORD YOUR FISHING SUCCESS)

Sport Fish of North America

☐ **Bass, Florida Largemouth** (Florida bass, bucketmouth, linesides, green trout, black bass, oswego bass)

Location: _____ Date: _____

Size:_____Comments: _____

☐ **Bass, Guadalupe** (black bass and guadalupe spotted bass)

Location: _____ Date: _____

Size:_____Comments: _____

☐ **Bass, Largemouth** (black bass, green bass, bigmouth, linesides, bucketmouth, northern largemouth)

Location: _____ Date: _____

Size:_____Comments: _____

☐ **Bass, Rock** (black perch, goggle-eye, rock sunfish)

Location: _____ Date: _____

Size:_____Comments: _____

☐ **Bass, Smallmouth** (black bass, smallie, redeye, brownie, brown bass, smallmouth, bronzeback)

Location: _____ Date: _____

Size:_____Comments: _____

☐ **Bass, Spotted** (Kentucky bass, spot, Alabama spotted bass)

Location: _____ Date: _____

Size:_____Comments: _____

☐ **Bass, Striped** (striper, rockfish, linesides)

Location: _____ Date: _____

Size:_____Comments: _____

☐ **Bass, White** (silver bass, striper, sand bass, whitey, dwarf striper)

Location: _____ Date: _____

Size: _____ Comments: _____

☐ **Bass, Yellow** (barfish, goldbass, yellowjacket, striped bass)

Location: _____ Date: _____

Size: _____ Comments: _____

☐ **Bluegill** (sun perch, bream, brim, blue sunfish, copper-belly, roach)

Location: _____ Date: _____

Size: _____ Comments: _____

☐ **Bullhead, Black** (catfish, black catfish, yellow belly bullhead)

Location: _____ Date: _____

Size: _____ Comments: _____

☐ **Bullhead, Brown** (squaretail, common bullhead, mudcat, brown catfish, bullpout, horned pout)

Location: _____ Date: _____

Size: _____ Comments: _____

☐ **Bullhead, Yellow** (yellow cat, creek cat, whitewhiskered bullhead)

Location: _____ Date: _____

Size: _____ Comments: _____

☐ **Carp, Common** (king carp)

Location: _____ Date: _____

Size: _____ Comments: _____

☐ **Catfish, Channel** (spotted cat, blue channel cat, great lakes catfish, lady cat, fiddler, spotted catfish)
Location: _____ Date: _____
Size:_____Comments: _____

☐ **Catfish, Flathead** (mud cat, yellow cat, shovelnose, pie cat)
Location: _____ Date: _____
Size:_____Comments: _____

☐ **Crappie, Black** (speckled perch, grass bass, papermou shiner, speckled bass)
Location: _____ Date: _____
Size:_____Comments: _____

☐ **Crappie, White** (papermouth, speckled perch, bachelor perch, silver bass, calico bass)
Location: _____ Date: _____
Size:_____Comments: _____

☐ **Drum, Red** (channel bass, redfish, spot-tail bass, red bass, red dorse, school drum, puppy drum)
Location: _____ Date: _____
Size:_____Comments: _____

☐ **Muskellunge** (muskie, lunge, maskinonge, great pike)
Location: _____ Date: _____
Size:_____Comments: _____

☐ **Perch, White** (silver bass, gray perch, sea perch, hump
Location: _____ Date: _____
Size:_____Comments: _____

☐ **Perch, Yellow** (ringed perch, striped perch, lake perch, jack perch)

Location: _____ Date: _____

Size:_____Comments: _____

☐ **Pickerel, Chain** (grass pike, duck-billed pike, jack, river pike, lake pickerel)

Location: _____ Date: _____

Size:_____Comments: _____

☐ **Pike, Northern** (great northern pike, jack, jackfish, pickerel, snake, gator)

Location: _____ Date: _____

Size:_____Comments: _____

☐ **Sailfish, Atlantic** (sailfish, sail, spikefish, spindlebeak, spindlesnoot, mylmeen)

Location: _____ Date: _____

Size:_____Comments: _____

☐ **Salmon, Atlantic** (landlocked salmon, ouananiche, sebago salmon, grilt, fiddler, grayling)

Location: _____ Date: _____

Size:_____Comments: _____

☐ **Salmon, Chinook** (king salmon, spring salmon, tyee, quinnat, blackmouth, blackjaw)

Location: _____ Date: _____

Size:_____Comments: _____

☐ **Salmon, Coho** (sea trout, silver salmon, hookbill, hooknose)

Location: _____ Date: _____

Size:_____Comments: _____

☐ **Salmon, Sockeye** (red salmon, blueback salmon, kokan salmon [landlocked form])
Location: _____ Date: _____
Size:_____Comments: _____

☐ **Sauger** (gray pike, river pike, jack, jackfish, sandpickerel
Location: _____ Date: _____
Size:_____Comments: _____

☐ **Sunfish, Green** (green perch, black perch, sand bass, creek perch)
Location: _____ Date: _____
Size:_____Comments: _____

☐ **Sunfish, Longear** (longear)
Location: _____ Date: _____
Size:_____Comments: _____

☐ **Sunfish, Pumpkinseed** (yellow sunfish, speckled perch, sunny, bream)
Location: _____ Date: _____
Size:_____Comments: _____

☐ **Sunfish, Redear** (yellow bream, bream, shellcracker)
Location: _____ Date: _____
Size:_____Comments: _____

☐ **Tarpon, Silver King** (silver king, silverfish, tarpum)
Location: _____ Date: _____
Size:_____Comments: _____

☐ **Trout, Apache** (Arizona trout)
Location: _____ Date: _____
Size:_____Comments: _____

☐ **Trout, Bonneville Cutthroat** (native trout, Utah trout, blue-head)

Location: _____ Date: _____

Size:_____Comments: _____

☐ **Trout, Brook** (eastern brook trout, brookie, speckled trout, native trout, squaretail, coaster, salter)

Location: _____ Date: _____

Size:_____Comments: _____

☐ **Trout, Brown** (brownie, river trout, brook trout, lake trout)

Location: _____ Date: _____

Size:_____Comments: _____

☐ **Trout, Cutthroat** (Clark's trout, native trout, cut, red-throat, mountain trout, black-spotted trout)

Location: _____ Date: _____

Size:_____Comments: _____

☐ **Trout, Golden** (kern river trout, mountain trout, goldie)

Location: _____ Date: _____

Size:_____Comments: _____

☐ **Trout, Greenback Cutthroat**

Location: _____ Date: _____

Size:_____Comments: _____

☐ **Trout, Lahontan Cutthroat** (native trout)

Location: _____ Date: _____

Size:_____Comments: _____

☐ **Trout, Lake** (landlocked salmon, bank trout, bumper, great gray trout, laker)

Location: _____ Date: _____

Size:_____Comments: _____

☐ **Trout, Rainbow** (steelhead, rainbow, redband trout, red-sides)

Location: _____ Date: _____

Size:_____Comments: _____

☐ **Trout, Rio Grande Cutthroat** (New Mexico cutthroat tro▮

Location: _____ Date: _____

Size:_____Comments: _____

☐ **Trout, Steelhead** (coastal rainbow trout, steelies, sea-rur rainbow)

Location: _____ Date: _____

Size:_____Comments: _____

☐ **Walleye** (walleyed pike, pickerel, jackfish, green pike)

Location: _____ Date: _____

Size:_____Comments: _____

☐ **Warmouth** (goggle-eye)

Location: _____ Date: _____

Size:_____Comments: _____

☐ **Weakfish** (tide runner, sea trout, yellow fin trout, yellow mouth, squeteague, gray)

Location: _____ Date: _____

Size:_____Comments: _____

GLOSSARY OF TERMS

Adaptation: A particular characteristic developed by a plant or animal that makes it better suited to its environment.

Air Bladder: A balloon-like organ in the gut area of a fish, which helps to regulate floatation and buoyancy. Also called "gas bladder" or "swim bladder."

Amphibians: Cold-blooded, smooth-skinned vertebrates that spend part of their life on land and part of their life in the water including frogs, toads, newts and salamanders.

Anadromous: Fish that spend most of their life in salt water but migrate to fresh water to spawn (reproduce).

Angler: A person who catches fish or attempts to catch fish for food or recreation.

Aquatic Insects: Insects that spend all or part of their lives in water e.g. mayflies.

Arthropod: Classification used to describe animals that do not have an internal backbone e.g. insects and crayfish.

Bait: Natural, processed and artificial objects used to catch fish. Examples of natural bait include worms, leeches and crickets. Examples of processed bait include bread, cheese, processed meat products and Powerbait. Artificial bait includes lures such as spoons, jigs, plugs, flies and spinners.

Barb: A sharp, spur-like projection near the pointed end of a hook.

Barbels: Whisker-like appendages with sensory capabilities found on some species including catfish and carp.

Behavior: The way an animal responds to its environment.

Biologist: A person who studies the science of living organisms and life processes.

Bobber: A surface float designed to support fishing tackle.

Bow: The forward portion of a boat.

C

Camouflage: A protective adaptation that enables a fish to disgu[...] itself or blend with its surroundings.

Carnivore: An animal that eats other animals; a meat eater.

Carrion: The body of a dead animal in the natural state of dec[...] which serves as a food source for some animals.

Catch-and-Release: Pertains to the practice of catching game[...] using sporting methods and releasing them alive a[...] unharmed. Catch-and-release is used as a wildlife managem[...] tool designed to increase fish populations by restricting [...] number of fish caught and kept by anglers as well as regulat[...] the size and type of the fish caught.

Cold-blooded (ectothermic): An animal whose body temperat[...] is dependent upon and varies with the temperature of its en[...] ronment e.g. fish, amphibians and reptiles.

Communication: Sound, scent or behavior recognized by me[...] bers of the same species. See also "pheromone" a[...] "courtship."

Competition: Two or more animals of the same or different spec[...] vying for the same space or sources of food.

Conservation officer: An employee of the government licensed [...] enforce wildlife laws.

Conservation: The care, wise use and management of a resour[...] such as rivers, fish or forests.

Consumer: Any organism that depends upon other organisr[...] dead or alive, for food.

Courtship: A behavior or series of actions an animal displays [...] indicate to the opposite sex that it is ready to mate in ord[...] to reproduce.

ver: Naturally-occurring sheltered areas that provide conceal-ment and shelter for wildlife such as a dead tree, fallen log, rock outcroppings, dense areas of brush or trees.

eel: A basket designed to carry fish, traditionally made of well-ventilated wicker.

el limit: The number and type of fish that can legally be caught during a given time.

ustacean: Freshwater and saltwater animals with a hard shell and jointed legs e.g. crayfish, lobster, shrimp and crab.

ology: The study of the relationships between living things and the environments in which they live.

osystem: An interacting system of plants, animals, soil and cli-matic conditions in a self-contained environment (e.g. pond, marsh, swamp, lake or stream).

dangered: A species in danger of becoming extinct due to declining population.

tuary: Area where fresh water and salt water meet.

hics: Principles of good conduct; a sense of right and wrong.

otic: A foreign species introduced to an area from another region or ecosystem, sometimes unintentionally. Exotic species are considered undesirable as they compete with native species for habitat and food. The zebra mussel is an example of a prob-lem exotic species.

tinct: A species that no longer exists.

ngerling: An immature fish. Also called "fry."

hery biologist: A person who manages aquatic and wetland habitats and fish reproduction and health.

Food chain: Plants and animals linked together as sources a consumers of food; typically an organism higher in the food ch eats one lower in the food chain, so the health of one is depe dent on the health of another.

Fresh water: A body of water that contains little salt e.g. pond, la or stream.

G

Gas bladder: See "air bladder."

Gaff: A large hook attached to a long pole used to retrieve fish.

H

Habitat enhancement: The development and improvement habitat (including sources of food, water, cover and space) the benefit of fish or wildlife.

Habitat: The local environment in which an animal live Components include food, water, cover (shelter) and space.

Headwater: The origin of a stream or river.

Herbivore: An animal that eats only plant material.

I

Ichthyology: The study of fish.

Instinct: An inherited or unlearned behavior of an animal.

Introduced species: A plant or animal brought from anoth region, often another continent, either intentionally or by ac dent; introduced species can have positive or negative effects the native species. Also referred to as "exotic" or "non-nativ especially when the result is negative.

Invertebrates: Animals without backbones, including insec crabs and crayfish (Arthropods), earthworms (Annelida) a jellyfish (Coelenterata).

L

Lateral line: A system of sensory nerves in the skin, which dete he movement of water and other fish. The lateral line extends om head to tail on either side of the fish.

ense: A state permit that allows a person to gather wild plants, unt, fish or trap.

iting factor: An environmental component such as drought, xtreme cold, shortage of food or cover which negatively impacts ildlife populations.

e: Artificial objects used to catch fish. Lures are artificial objects ade of fur, wood, feathers, metal, plastic, rubber and nylon esigned and made to resemble natural bait (e.g. insects or orms).

mmal: A warm-blooded animal that has fur or hair and pro-uces milk to feed its young.

gration: The seasonal movements of fish and wildlife from one rea to another, usually triggered by length of daylight hours.

t: The semen of a male fish that fertilizes the female's eggs dur-g spawning.

llusk: Freshwater and saltwater invertebrates with smooth soft odies, including clams, snails and oysters.

ltiple-use: Using and managing an area of land to provide nore than one benefit simultaneously such as timber harvest, ildlife habitat, outdoor recreation and watershed management.

tive: An indigenous or naturally occurring species of plant or nimal.

tural resource: Materials found in nature to which people have ssigned value such as timber, fresh water, wildlife and fossil uels (coal and oil).

nivore: An animal that eats both plants and animals (meat).

Opportunist: An animal that can take advantage of any numbe[r] food sources available.

P

Panfish: Small freshwater sport fish that can be fried whole pan, including crappie, sunfish, perch and bass.

Pheromone: A chemical scent secreted as a means of comm[uni]cation between members of the same species.

Photosynthesis: A series of chemical changes in which pl[ants] combine sunlight, gasses and water to form sugar or food.

Plankton: Microscopic plants and animals that are eaten by and other aquatic life.

Poacher: A person who takes fish or wildlife illegally.

Pollution: Toxic (poisonous) substances deposited in the air, w[ater] or soil creating an unhealthy environment.

Predator: An animal that hunts and feeds on other animals (pr[ey])

Prey: An animal hunted or killed for food by other animals (pre[da]tors).

Producer: Refers to plants that obtain energy from the sun a[nd] produce food through the process of photosynthesis.

R

Range: The particular geographic region in which a specie[s is] found.

Recreation: An activity undertaken for enjoyment; entertainm[ent] often associated with natural resources (water, forests, rock [for]mations) includes rock climbing, bird watching, fishi[ng] canoeing and hunting.

Redd: A nest-like depression made by a male or female fish contain eggs.

Renewable natural resource: A natural resource that can [be] replenished and harvested including trees and wildlife.

tile: A cold-blooded vertebrate animal that lays eggs (e.g. snakes, lizards and turtles).

arian area: Lands adjacent to streams, rivers, lakes and other wetlands where the vegetation is influenced by the great availability of water.

t water: A body of water with a high concentration of salt (e.g. oceans and seas).

venger: An animal that feeds on the remains of dead animals.

ool: A group of fish.

son: Time of year when game species may be legally harvested.

ker: A small metal weight used by anglers designed to sink bait or lures.

wning: The process of fish reproduction; involves females laying eggs and males fertilizing them to produce young fish; sometimes the adults build a redd.

cies: A group of animals that have similar structure, common ancestors and characteristics they maintain through breeding.

rt fish: Certain species of fish that are actively pursued by anglers because they are considered challenging and/or fun to catch or they are desirable to eat. Examples include bass, walleye, trout and salmon. Also referred to as "gamefish."

rtsmanship: Lawful and ethical behavior demonstrated by hunters, anglers or trappers.

rn: The back of a boat.

wardship: Responsible care of natural resources for future generations.

cking: The purposeful and artificial propagation and introduction of game species into an area. The Brook Trout is an example of a species that is stocked.

Stress: A factor that may negatively affect an animal's health s
as lack of food, disease or overpopulation; stress may also re
in adaptation by the animal.

T

Tackle: Fishing equipment e.g. rods, reels, poles, line, sink
hooks, bobbers and lures.

Territory: The area a fish will defend against intruders of its c
species, especially during breeding season.

Threatened: A classification for wildlife species whose popula
is in great decline and approaching the "endangered" clas
cation.

Trespassing: Entering onto another person's land without perr
sion.

Trolling: A common method of fishing in which bait or lures
pulled through the water behind a slow moving boat.

V

Vertebrate: Animals with backbones including fish, birds, ma
mals and reptiles.

W

Warm-blooded (endothermic): An animal whose body tempe
ture is unrelated to its environment (e.g. mammals and bird

Wildlife agency: A state or federal organization responsible
managing wildlife.

Wildlife management: A combination of techniques, scien
knowledge and technical skills used to protect, conserve a
manage wildlife and habitat.

Wildlife: Publicly owned, non-domesticated plants and anim
(including mammals, birds, fish, reptiles, insects and amp
ians).

Winter kill: The death of animals or plants during winter resul
from lack of food and exposure to cold.

IGHLIGHTS OF WILDLIFE FOREVER'S ATIONAL FISHERIES PROJECTS

scription of Projects

- Improved fish habitat in Flint Creek in **Alabama's** Wheeler National Wildlife Refuge.

- Purchased 160 acres of land near Humpy Creek on Kodiak Island in **Alaska**, protecting important salmon habitat

- Constructed and installed 3,000 bass shelters, 2,520 catfish houses and 150 tire towers in **Arizona's** Lake Havasu

- Restored native Channel Catfish to the Buffalo River in **Arkansas**.

- Assisted students at **California's** Casa Grande High School in the restoration of seven miles of Adobe Creek

- Restored fish habitat along a 1.5-mile stretch of the North Fork of the Gunnison River in **Colorado**.

- Tagged tens of thousands of billfish off the coast of **Florida** and throughout the world to study migration and other crucial information

- Assisted in the creation of a fish hatchery at **Hawaii's** Wahiawa Intermediate School

- Improved conditions for cutthroat and bull trout in **Idaho's** Cougar Creek by restoring stream to its natural channel profile

- Raised and released millions of walleye and sauger fry plus hundreds of thousands of fingerlings into the **Illinois** River

- Installed an aeration system on Five Island Lake in **Iowa**.

- Placed 167 artificial fish habitat structures in Lake Perry in **Kansas**.

- Created pools to improve fish habitat by installing 16 deflectors in the north fork of Little River in **Kentucky**

- Improved 3,500 feet of stream habitat on **Michigan's** Bige Creek by installing eight habitat improvement structures

- Purchased new aerator and repaired three others and plac them in **Minnesota's** O'Dowd Lake to prevent winter kill

- Placed 100 artificial fish habitat structures in **Missou** Truman Reservoir

- Stabilized three miles of streams and restored 12 miles riparian habitat within **Montana's** Centennial Valley

- Restored bull trout migration and spawning habitat **Nevada's** Jack Creek by replacing existing culvert with prefabricated bridge

- Reintroduced native walleye into the St. Lawrence Ri Valley in **New York**

- Treated and removed Brazilian Elodea from Slade's Lake **South Carolina**

- Purchased equipment to supply water to six ponds p ducing crappie, bass and catfish for the Choke Cany Reservoir in **Texas**

- Purchased fish rearing tanks and weight scales for renov ing the Brook Trout hatchery on Lake Seymour in **Vermo**

- Constructed and installed an interpretive exhibit on mou tain trout fisheries at **Virginia's** Mount Rogers Natio Recreation Area

- Improved a salmon hatchery in **Washington** by replac pipelines and adding new space to expand rearing capabi

- Improved streams through small dam removal on t Deerskin River and the Milwaukee River in **Wisconsin**

- Created a watchable wildlife area in Buffalo, **Wyoming**, t includes a warmwater fishery containing crappies, ba and perch